EVERY

THING

WORTH

HAVING

ANOTHER DESTINY IMAGE BOOK BY EUGENE LUNING

Yesterday, Today, and Forever: A Journey Through 30 Unchangeable Promises of God

EVERY

a journey through

THING

30 unchangeable promises

WORTH

from the mouth of God

HAVING

EUGENE LUNING

DESTINY IMAGE® PUBLISHERS, INC.
P.O. Box 310, Shippensburg, PA 17257-0310
"Promoting Inspired Lives."

This book and all other Destiny Image and Destiny Image Fiction books are available at Christian bookstores and distributors worldwide.

Cover design by: Christian Rafetto

For more information on foreign distributors, call 717-532-3040.

Reach us on the Internet: www.destinyimage.com.

ISBN 13 TP: 978-0-7684-5756-8

ISBN 13 eBook: 978-0-7684-5757-5

For Worldwide Distribution.

1 2 3 4 5 6 7 8 / 24 23 22 21 20

"We know sorrow, yet our joy is inextinguishable. We have 'nothing to bless ourselves with' yet we bless many others with true riches. We are penniless, and yet in reality we have everything worth having."

—2 Corinthians 6:10 (Phillips)

*   *   *   *   *   *   *

"But is it really possible, amid the wear and tear of daily life, to walk in the experience of these blessings? Are they really meant for all God's children? Let us rather ask the question, Is it possible for God to do what He has promised?"

—Andrew Murray, *The Two Covenants*

To Hadley.

To Tripp.

To Hoyt.

CONTENTS

PROLOGUE

Because the book in your hands is the second of two volumes on "the promises from the mouth of God," I won't reiterate the first volume's self-explanation and Foreword. Instead, I'll ask you a few pointed, personal questions:

- Are you presently totally satisfied with your experience of God?

- Do you feel as intimate with Him as you think it's humanly possible to feel?

- Do you believe that you can trust His personal promises implicitly?

If not, why not?

Because, if God is totally true and trustworthy—all-knowing and perfectly lovely in action, word and work—and if He has already done absolutely everything necessary, in Heaven and on earth, to set you free—everything including not sparing His very own Son from gruesome death—and if He has made direct, He-to-you promises of spiritual satisfaction, earthly intimacy, power by His Spirit, and practical provision for your human life—*then what are you waiting for?*

For Him to become somehow more true and trustworthy?

To intellectually assent more fully to His loveliness?

To shore up your "theological position" regarding His death for you?

For some better logical understanding of His eternal plan for satisfaction, intimacy, power, and personal provision?

You might be waiting a very long time!

But what if—

—God being Truth—

—utterly lovely; in fact, Love Himself—

—having done everything *already* to make you free forever and ever—

—having made direct, personal promises for your spiritual, earthly, heavenly life—

—you simply took Him at His word?

Wouldn't that be the life He'd actually want for you?

It would be.

And here it is.

Let's go explore.

EUGENE LUNING
COLORADO SPRINGS, COLORADO
JUNE, 2020

Section One

WALKING WITH JESUS

Promise

1

"...And remember, I am with you always, to the end of the age."

MATTHEW 28:20 HCSB

Do you know what's maybe most interesting about any "end of an age"? It never seems to recognize that it's inhabiting an end of an age. Historically speaking, every era and epoch—even if it's poised at the edge of a precipice—always receives its reality as the simple cycling of the days. Its people get out of bed, look in the mirror, brush their teeth, get dressed, have breakfast, say goodbye to their family, go off to work. They finish work, come home, take off their work clothes, get comfortable, have dinner, entertain themselves, get ready for bed, fall asleep. And, tomorrow—*tomorrow!*—might arrive the new reality that cuts them off from the old reality: the *"end of the age"* was today. Tomorrow—*tomorrow!*—might be the day of the Great Market Crash of 1929, the arrival of the Prussians to the edges of Paris, Alexander the Great meeting the High Priest of Israel on a prospect near Jerusalem.

The most interesting thing about "the end of the age" is that, quite reasonably speaking, you might be living through its last moments—right now. You might be one who wakes on the morrow, finds the former ruling reality no longer ruling, and thinks, *Oh! So that was it, I guess...*

In a similar way (and paraphrasing one of my favorite lines from Hemingway, here) the beauty within a revolutionary army is that, if you follow its flank far enough, it always ends with just one person. There is one final man or woman, ready in their foxhole or in their observation post, who, knowing it or not, is the last line—the farthest flank—of the whole endeavor. And, realizing it or not, their presence there—sitting, waiting, ready, observing, armed—might have outsize impact within the bulk of the whole army. They might be the tip of the spear, for all they know.

Now today's promise:

What if today is the literal "end of the age"—the end of everything you've ever known—and what if *you* are the one at the Kingdom Army's outer arm? What if your day today was the *exact* plan of God for establishing His Way within that *one* heart, that *one* situation, that *one* city block? Right now, watching you, watching your day ahead, what if the whole of Heaven—angels and saints—are holding their breath for the heavenly outcome they *hope* will happen? What if you learned to align the movements of your day today with the seriousness, and potential *non-serialness*, of the day, the week, the year, the age?

Again, what if today *is* the end of the age?

Again, what if *you* are "the one" for someone?

"Remember, I am with you always," Jesus says to you, meaning each one of those words, "to the very end of the age"—eternal age or *any* age. The One who sits on the throne of Heaven, and within the movements of your human heart, is the One whose promise you have for *any* end of *any* age. He is the very One who already accomplished His own one-man, revolutionary-army-action to rescue *your* heart from sin, death, and the grave. He is the One who ushered in the ultimate New, Final Age of human history—the glorious end of the Old Covenant—when He calmly strode from the open grave. Jesus is Himself the farthest flank of the age-old Way; He is Himself the "Alpha and Omega" of ages, eras, eternity: His presence is Heaven itself.

And remember, I—that presence, that power, that Way—*am with you always, to the end of the age.*

Jesus, the One who's already done everything on earth and in Heaven to set you free, is the One who's with you today—in Heaven and on earth. Jesus, that wonderful Man from Nazareth, is the One who's made this promise—*forever*—whether today is "it" or not, whether you are "the one" or not.

Remember: Jesus is with you today.

And to the end of the age.

Every single day.

Promise
2

"For this is what the high and exalted One says—he who lives forever, whose name is holy: 'I live in a high and holy place, but also with the one who is contrite and lowly in spirit, to revive the spirit of the lowly and to revive the heart of the contrite. I will not accuse them forever, nor will I always be angry, for then they would faint away because of me—the very people I have created. I was enraged by their sinful greed; I punished them, and hid my face in anger, yet they kept on in their willful ways. I have seen their ways, but I will heal them; I will guide them and restore comfort to Israel's mourners, creating praise on their lips....'"

ISAIAH 57:15-19 NIV

As you took the time to slowly read those words, did you hear both the past and present elements in play, the way that God was pointing at both the Old and New Covenants at the same time? If I were to rearrange the verses of this promise, putting them into sequential covenantal order, it might read something like this:

The very people I have created, I was enraged by their sinful greed; I punished them, and hid my face in anger, yet they kept on in their willful ways... I will not accuse them forever, nor will I always be angry, for then they would faint away because of me... I have seen their ways, but I will heal them; I will guide them and restore comfort to Israel's mourners, creating praise on their lips... I live in a high and holy place, but also with the one who is contrite and lowly in spirit, to revive the spirit of the lowly and to revive the heart of the contrite.

In that ordering, consider the component parts—especially with reference to all that Jesus has already accomplished for us:

"The very people I have created..." Remember: You are a creation. All of humanity, all of everything everywhere, everything we know and can see all around us, all of it was first the thought of God before it was spoken into existence by the Word—the Creative Exhalation—who is Jesus. We are "the very people" whom He formed out of nothing.

"...I was enraged by their sinful greed; I punished them, and hid my face in anger, yet they kept on in their willful ways." In other words, we "fell." We are fallen. Mankind is irrevocably broken. The first man, tempted by the "sinful greed" to be like, and become, and *to be* God, ended up dashing us all to the ground. And our punishment was nothing other than the fruit of the tree of the knowledge of good and evil: the endless razor's edge we walk between our image-of-Godness and

our now-inborn sin. And yet, for all human history until the arrival of the Savior, we "kept on in our willful ways."

But: *"I will not accuse them forever, nor will I always be angry, for then they would faint away because of me..."* His prophetic promises were then offered up to mankind. Wild-eyed seers would appear within Israel's midst and would speak of the redemption on the way. Prophets like Isaiah, the mouthpiece here. Bringing hope and a future.

"I have seen their ways, but I will heal them; I will guide them and restore comfort to Israel's mourners, creating praise on their lips." Did you catch the opening word of that declaration? "I"—"*I* have seen their ways..." The very God who had created us, felt enraged by our sin, punished us, hid His face from our ongoingly willful ways; who had consciously chosen not to accuse us forever, nor to always be angry because of our weakness...*He arrived to us!* He crossed the border. He "saw our ways" with a human eye. He physically reached out with a human hand that was His own to touch and restore flesh that was ours: *He healed us.* He spoke perfect words with His perfect human intellect and wisdom that are perfectly able to lead us: *He guided us.* He knowingly went to a death for which we were marked and, even, destined and deserving: *He restored comfort and life to us.* He rose from the grave to set the human heart free from fear and death: *He created an everlasting praise for our lips.*

And now? Where is He now?

"I live in a high and holy place..." He ascended. He ascended—*for us.* As a Man, as the perfectly righteous, having-redeemed-the-flesh-by-obedience-in-life-and-death New

Man, He went right back to the Father. He took the human body He'd taken on back to the throne room of Heaven, so that mankind would always have a perfect Advocate there. He ascended—*for us*. And walking back into the throne room, with the angels and saints overwhelmed with His glory, He retook the throne from which He'd made everything. He turned to the Father, exchanged an all-knowing glance with Him, and resumed the perfect rule He'd always had. That's where He lives now.

"...***But also*** *with the one who is contrite and lowly in spirit, to revive the spirit of the lowly and to revive the heart of the contrite.*" You see, ten short days after His heavenward ascension, there occurred the greatest cataclysmic event since the God-Man Incarnation: *the God-mankind Inhabitation.* The Holy Spirit of God, sent at the express wish of both the Father and the Son, suddenly filled the hearts of contrite, lowly people like us. God was there—in Heaven, in the throne room, on the throne— and now here—in the hearts of His people.

My friend, the promise of this promise is that, not only does He know you; not only does He know your sin; not only has He promised full redemption; not only has He arrived— perfectly human, perfectly relatable—to do the work to heal and guide you; not only has He died to set you free; not only has He risen to arm your lips with praise; not only has He ascended to Heaven for you—He has forever taken His immovable, unshakable seat upon the throne of Heaven, *for you*, and, *in you*, has come to live forever! The dual-residency of Jesus is the promise, here. Those two places He is alive and active—for you.

Today, what if you talked to Him, walked with Him, in full remembrance and recognition that He's *there* and *right here?*

My friend, truly, He has done it!

He is everything you need—and right where you need Him to be!

Promise
3

"But He said to me, 'My grace is sufficient for you, for My power is perfected in weakness....'"

2 Corinthians 12:9 BSB

You may already know the context of this promise, as spoken to Paul, of his debilitating "thorn in the flesh"—probably some crippling physical ailment or injury—and his three-times ask for God to remove it from his life and ministry (2 Corinthians 12:7-9). But, instead, he receives grace. He receives, rather than what he immediately desired, precisely what *the Lord* desired, because the Lord is looking at the whole story as a whole. The entirety of human history, to Him, is intelligible. And the part each of us play in His plan is perfectly suited to each of us. Paul, physically weak, unable to rely on the forcefulness of his own power and personality, was the instrument Jesus used almost more than any other.

So, let's look at this promise for ourselves:

What are the variables we would seem to bring to the table, if we want to personally experience the same sort of life of usefulness that Paul lived?

- Ability to listen and hear from Jesus: *"But He said to me…"*

- Willingness to conform unto a godly contentment: *"My grace is sufficient for you…"*

- Our acknowledgment and acceptance that we are, in fact, weak: *"for My power is perfected in weakness."*

And just so you internalize this, everything I just wrote down—all three of those Pauline requirements—are completely counterposed to the ways of the world you're living in. The world will think you're crazy for striving to hear words from a 2,000-years-ago Carpenter-Teacher; it will scoff at your almost Stoic attempts to find peace in a simple godly contentment; it will find nothing more reprehensible than a surrender unto acknowledgment of weakness, an acceptance that a greater heavenly power is thus activated.

But, assuming you see the life of Paul-following-Jesus to be as thrilling as I do, let's take a look at the fruit that will be borne from the Godward direction:

- He promises to personally speak to us: Again, *"He said to me…"*

- He promises a grace that's greater than our stated, or unstated, need: *"My grace is sufficient for you…"*

- He promises, in place of our weakness, dynamic experience of His power being perfected within ourselves: *"My power is perfected in weakness."*

In contemplating on so hearing from Him, finding peace in Him, experiencing the joy of His promised power arriving, I'm reminded of one of my greatest heroes of belief. In fact, the whole idea of these writings was partially inspired by his own experience of looking for promises, holding them out to God, and then waiting upon His answer. This particular hero is named George Müller, the 19th-century evangelist and director of miraculously-provided-for orphanages in Bristol, England.

From the earliest dawn of his personal belief in Jesus, it was his desire to trust Jesus unreservedly for practical provision and finance. Müller refused, simply, to "ask any man." When he—and his eventual thousands of orphans—needed food, he prayed and waited. And the results—always—year after year—for a lifetime—were hearing from the Lord, sufficiency from the Lord, and high, glorious experiences of the power of the Lord "perfected in weakness."

At some length, I want you to read what a friend of Müller's, Arthur Pierson, wrote about his total attachment to the promises of God. Consider deeply—this is beautiful:

> George Müller stored up reasons for God's intervention. As he came upon promises, authorized declarations of God concerning Himself, names and titles He had chosen to express and reveal His true nature and will, injunctions and invitations which gave to the believer a right to pray and boldness in supplication—as he saw all these, fortified and exemplified by the instances of prevailing

prayer, he laid these arguments up in memory, and then on occasions of great need brought them out and spread them before a prayer-hearing God. It is pathetically beautiful to follow this humble man of God into the secret place, and there hear him pouring out his soul in these argumentative pleadings, as though he would so order his cause before God as to convince Him that He must interpose to save His own name and word from dishonor!

These were *His* orphans, for had He not declared Himself the Father of the fatherless? This was *His* work, for had He not called His servant to do His bidding, and what was that servant but an instrument that could neither fit itself nor use itself? … And if this were God's work, was He not bound to care for His own work? And was not all this deliberately planned and carried on for His own glory? And would He suffer His own glory to be dimmed? Had not His own word been given and confirmed by His oath, and could God allow His promise, thus sworn, to be dishonored even in the least particular? Were not the half-believing church and the unbelieving world looking on, to see how the Living God would stand by His own unchanging assurance, and would He supply an argument for the skeptic and the scoffer? Would He not, must He not, rather put new proofs of His faithfulness in the mouth of His saints, and furnish increasing arguments wherewith to silence the cavilling tongue and put to shame the hesitating disciple?[1]

My friend, let us be *totally unhesitating* in listening for Jesus and His personal promises; let us be *totally believing* in the joy of finding our life in Him; let us use this day—every minute of this day—to acknowledge and accept that the places of our weakness are the *precise places* we may wait upon His perfect strength.

You are allowed to hold up His promises for a righteous argumentation.

You are meant to live on His promises—and to live from them.

Endnote

1. Arthur T. Pierson, *George Müller of Bristol: His Life of Prayer and Faith* (Grand Rapids, MI: Kregel Publications, 1999).

Promise

4

"Because he holds fast to me in love, I will deliver him; I will protect him, because he knows my name. When he calls to me, I will answer him; I will be with him in trouble; I will rescue him and honor him. With long life I will satisfy him and show him my salvation."

PSALM 91:14-16 ESV

There's no time like the present—especially a present concurrent with a worldwide pandemic—for considering the relationship between cause and effect. But, truth be told, I have always been fascinated by cause and effect. It interests me to watch how certain actions, movements, or words can have such immediate, verifiable results in such immediately observable ways. And then, by repetition, to see the same thing happening over and over again, I can understand the draw empiricists and scientists feel toward their work. It's a satisfying thing to test and come to know the make-up of a cause; it must be thrilling to begin to understand its direct relationship with some noted effect.

While, today, we're feeling the fear of a cause and its obvious effect on people and society, it's a beautiful thing to know that men and women all around the world are, as I'm writing, fighting to comprehend the cause and effect behind this particularly insidious virus. (In fact, if you happen to be one of them and are reading these words, now or in the future, *thank you!* I'm overwhelmed with gratitude that you studiously, day by day, fought for all our lives and livelihoods.)

Now with that said, why am I talking about cause and effect?

Because, in all these varied promises, this may be the one—or, really, the ones—where God Himself most clearly points at a series of causes and effects. And get ready for what I'm about to say. In them, the God of the universe, the One who created everything, the Trinity of unbridled power, tells us that, actually, *we are a cause with heavenly effect!* We can act in ways where *He has already told us the result that will follow.*

Pay close attention:

- If you *hold fast to Him in love,* what happens? He *"will deliver"* you.

- If you *know His name* for yourself, what occurs? He *"will protect"* you.

- If you take the time to *call to Him,* what has He promised to do? He *"will answer"* you.

- If you *call to Him* in trouble, what will He immediately provide for you? His presence, His *"rescue,"* His *"honor."*

- If you make a constant habit, each day, of constantly calling upon Him, what will be

the empirically verifiable, heavenly-earthly
result? An experience of *"long life"* with Him,
no matter the number of years you inhabit;
delight in possessing His salvation *"on earth as
it is in Heaven."*

Isn't it an absolutely amazingly overwhelmingly astounding thought that your life today is the earthly cause to Heaven's effect? You can simply, subtly, literally, realistically take little moments today and shape the actions and decisions and processes of the throne room of Heaven! Doesn't that sound a little more interesting than anything you currently have planned?

So, again, what would be the actions this promise promises are the actions required to act as that earthly cause to Heaven's effect?

Read again:

- Hold fast to Him in love today.
- Know His name—and Him—for yourself.
- Call to Him all throughout today.
- Call to Him in trouble.
- Keep calling.
- Call upon this One who is your Savior.

What do you think? Are those behaviors possible today? Can you actually imagine yourself simply completing those actions?

Then, get ready:

- He *will* deliver you.
- He *will* protect you.

- He *will* answer your entreaties.
- He *will* be with you.
- He *will* rescue you and honor you.
- He *will* satisfy, save you, and show you the salvation that is an experience—*today*—of your eternity—*to come*—with Him.

And all these causes and effects have been promised you. Amen and amen.

Promise
5

"Don't be afraid, for I am with you. Don't be discouraged, for I am your God. I will strengthen you and help you. I will hold you up with my victorious right hand."

Isaiah 41:10 NLT

Imagine if you were sitting in prison—but not some comfortable, modern, reasonably reasonable prison—you're sitting on cold, wet stones with rats scurrying around the floor and between your legs; the only single "window" in your cell is just a slit in the door that leads back into the inner hallway. The only sounds you can hear are the occasional openings and shuttings—*BANG!*—of the huge iron and wood doors of the various cells. Well, actually, sometimes you can hear the groanings of beaten prisoners, feeble attempts to communicate by tapping along the adjoining cell walls; and, of course, there's the constant water-torturing sound of the *drip-drip-dripping* of the ceiling making your cell-floor as wet as it is.

Do you have a sense of the type of environment I'm thinking of?

Well, on a particular night—though let's be honest, for you there are no particularities between day and night, night and day: all are the same—something *seems* different. It all began long after the delivery of the disgusting pot of gruel they call your evening meal: an arrival of two prisoners. You could hear the guards talking loudly.

"Did you like that?" they shouted at the prisoners, laughing.

"The finest flogging I ever saw," the other said.

You walked to the slit in your door and watched the two and two pass—two guards and two prisoners. These new prisoners looked like somewhat regular men; their bearing upright and proud; their cloaks draped over their crooked arms. Both their backs and shoulders and upper arms were totally flayed open: the skin hanging in shreds, blood still wet and pouring down.

Who are these men? you wonder. They'd clearly gotten a worse one than almost anyone you'd ever seen…

Then, the screeching of the hinge of a cell door…

Then—BANG!—the familiar sound of it slamming shut.

As you sat back down to try to find your comfort for the night, you continued to wonder about those two men down the way. How had they so offended the authorities to get what they got? They didn't seem to look the type.

Then, hours passed.

Something woke you.

You listen for the sound.

There it goes again.

Singing!

"You are good, You are holy, You are worthy...Jesus...You are good, You are holy, You are worthy...Jesus..."

And as you're sitting there on the dank, disgusting floor of the cell of the prison you're scheduled to die in, listening to the sound of this singing and the strangely wonderful sound of that name—"Jesus"—*you begin to feel the floor moving beneath you!* A rumbling beginning deep, deep down in the bowels of the earth is rising up, up, up into the structure of the prison. You feel the stones beneath you starting to shake, the upper timbers of the ceiling are cracking and bowing—*suddenly the door of your cell slams open inwardly!*

Instantly, you are on your feet.

You are already in the hallway. It's been weeks since you've walked anywhere other than around your small cell.

But, surprising yourself, instead of turning right toward the outside world—you're turning left. You must walk the three doors down and ask those men, "Who is Jesus?" and "How is He so good, holy, and worthy to merit your song?"

*　　*　　*

On that night from Acts 16, Paul and Silas didn't know about the mechanics of the earthquake, the jailer, their eventual deliverance. They didn't know—the way we modern readers do—that, by the next day, they'd be walking out the gates of that now-ruined prison.

Here's what they did know: *"Don't be afraid, for I am with you. Don't be discouraged, for I am your God. I will strengthen you and help you. I will hold you up with my victorious right hand."*

If I may be bold, your circumstances today can't hold a candle to the circumstances those two apostles encountered at midnight in Philippi. They had been wrongly accused, beaten, thrown in an inner cell; their feet were stocked; they might not live out the morrow.

Yet, finding themselves potentially at death's door, immobilized with nowhere to go, nothing to do, I imagine them looking at each other, smiling, nodding, and beginning their song. And this midnight worship at Philippi, in prison, doesn't only set off an earthly earthquake: it gives us insight into the ever-available heavenly glories of what it means to trust the power of Jesus always. It shows us that no matter what today holds, you and I can trust today's promise and see the *"victorious right hand"* of our God. It tells us that our greatest, best, first (or final) recourse should be worship; that there's nothing that can stop our wondrous Lord.

Do you believe today's promise?

Do you believe today's promise—*for yourself?*

Because, on the other end of your weakest, feeblest, last-ditch try at trusting Him is the Jesus who obliterated the prison at Philippi. On the other end of your whispered, unsure prayer is the Man who conquered death and shattered the wall between this life and the next one.

On the other side of your worship stands Jesus.

Will you trust Him for this day?

Promise

6

"Come to Me, all you who labor and are heavy laden, and I will give you rest. Take My yoke upon you and learn from Me, for I am gentle and lowly in heart, and you will find rest for your souls. For My yoke is easy and My burden is light."

MATTHEW 11:28-30 NKJV

Although this certainly seems like one of the most gentle, peaceful-sounding, deep-breath-inducing promises in the Gospels, I want to take it in a totally different direction. Indeed, in place of how it usually makes you feel, I want to make a series of bold declarations that I want you to take hold of today.

Bold Declaration 1: It is for you to come and take this promise.

Look at the verbs Jesus uses as He explains our part in the inheritance of these words: *come, take, learn, find.* Those are action verbs—powerful, positive, forward-moving activities. He is inviting you to *do* things. He wants you to use the course of the day ahead to physically change your direction and path, and to *come* to Him instead of anyone else. He wants you to stand before Him, eye to eye, and to *take* what He's telling you is rightfully yours—no one else's. He then wants you to sit down at His feet—you're not yet on the same level—and to practically *learn* His Way as a proper disciple. Then He wants today—and every day—to find you in the joyous, exploratory process of *finding* His rest, His will, His delight, His face.

Bold Declaration 2: Jesus is waiting for you to come and get it.

Look at the words He uses as He describes the posture and positioning *He* is taking with reference to the words of this promise: *give, rest, gentle, lowly in heart, easy, light*. Does He sound like some sort of taskmaster to you? Does He talk like this process of exchange is going to be arduous or overly involved? Is there any part of reading these words—*give, rest, gentle, lowly in heart, easy, light*—that makes you think He is anything less than overjoyed at the prospect of your arrival to receive His offer? He wants to *give* you His rest. The eyes of Jesus are *gentle* and show that He is *lowly in heart*. The work that He will call you to do is between you and Him; you will absolutely find it to be *easy* and *light*. He guarantees it.

Bold Declaration 3: We've been reading this promise wrong for too long.

Too often, I have heard this promise preached on like it's somehow natural and normal that Christians are feeling *heavy laden* and that this whole thing feels like *labor*. Wrong and wrong, I'd tell you! That is not the position we *ever should've been in!*

In fact, let this promise correct your interpretation of the whole Christian life, if you've ever been in the camp of the working hard, thinking you're earning your way to anything at all. The life of following Jesus is meant to be costly, not hard; it is He who does the work of the entirety of the everything that's ever needed. This promise isn't about the weary, heavy-laden, laboriously living, endlessly groaning sorts who struggle and strain to, finally, let down their guard. This promise is about Jesus. And His Way. It's an invitation into the life He Himself led.

Bold Declaration 4: The work of Jesus is rest—His rest is the work.

When a man or woman *comes* to Jesus of Nazareth, takes the *rest* He is offering, finds His yoke to be *light and easy*, and *learns* from Him, that man or woman then enters into a load-sharing, mutually yoked work that is all Jesus, all the time, along His restful Way. No longer does that man or woman require the self-justification of pointing to their religious exhaustion as proof of their self-salvation. They can simply turn their head a little—under the yoke with Jesus—and absolutely delight that He is actually doing it all. He is pulling the whole weight of the whole Christian life. He is carving out new fields for simple planting of seeds. He is showing us how to plant those seeds most fruitfully. He is teaching us to take our noonday meal in the shade of yonder tree. He instructs us as we take each step by step. He is laughing at the mistakes we make along the way. He is pointing back over our shoulder at the work almost unconsciously done. And He'll turn us for Home when the work is, at last, completed.

Jesus says, *"Come to Me, all you who labor and are heavy laden, and I will give you rest. Take My yoke upon you and learn from Me, for I am gentle and lowly in heart, and you will find rest for your souls. For My yoke is easy and My burden is light."*

Thank You, Jesus.

Promise
7

"Don't you have a saying, 'It's still four months until harvest?' I tell you, open your eyes and look at the fields! They are ripe for harvest. Even now the one who reaps draws a wage and harvests a crop for eternal life, so that the sower and the reaper may be glad together. Thus the saying 'One sows and another reaps' is true. I sent you to reap what you have not worked for. Others have done the hard work, and you have reaped the benefits of their labor."

JOHN 4:35-38 NIV

I want you to think of a certain individual, born on a certain day, in a certain town, to a certain mother, and raised in the particularly certain way they were raised. This individual had a fairly typical childhood, filled with most of the same normalcies as everyone else—school, teachers, friends, and extracurriculars. Week by week, this person learned things, finished the days, enjoyed experiences of home and family, had dreams, came up with adventures and pursued them. The earliest childhood of this individual was probably a lot like yours. There were ups and downs, of course; but on balance, the whole was fairly fine, comfortable, normal.

Getting older, the person we're considering went through all the additional complexities of getting older—more feelings and emotions, friends changing, etc. Life took on an aspect that they'd never fully considered—that not everyone you meet is categorically good or kind or "for you" in the conduct of their own lives. So, let it be said: the rest of adolescence, and up into early-adulthood for our individual was—again, on balance—quite a good experience of the human existence. They felt mostly noticed, seen, safe, certainly provided for, not too worried; they felt that they had friends enough, smarts enough, all that.

Now let's get to the important event in this individual's life.

At some point—and our individual would've had trouble enumerating the exact days and times—they began to have some experience of, some awareness of, some interest in, the presence and reality of God. It was almost like He'd hovered right at the edge of this person's experience of reality and, here and there, made practical incursions right into it. Our individual "felt something," they might've said. They began sensing that there was maybe more to life.

And that was when they finally, actually heard for the very first time that wonderful description of, and the name, Jesus. They heard that He had already arrived upon the earth. They heard that He had paid the price to set them free. They heard that He had come back from the dead. They heard that actual relationship was actually, truly available.

So our individual, on a certain day, at a certain place, at a certain time, had their particularly certain way of praying to Jesus for the very first time. They prayed a prayer of salvation, of repentance. They asked that Jesus would look across the breadth of their life—everything that had come before—and that He'd both forgive and use the past for His own present and future glory. Our individual gave over their life to Jesus.

And—did you know this?—Jesus instantly gave them a new life. Like on the very first day, born on a certain day, in a certain town, to a certain mother, our individual was re-born on a certain day, in a certain town, to a certain heavenly *Father.* They were made new—*forever.* They were now ready to stand before the Father—*holy and blameless.* They were beloved of Jesus—*no matter what.* They'd been eternally redeemed— *for something.*

What had our individual been chosen for? What was the new purpose of their redeemed human existence? Why had Jesus, looking down from the throne room of Heaven, before and within the seeming constructs of time, appointed *our* individual both for salvation and for a steady, daily discipleship?

That, no matter their particular circumstances—whether existential or in this particular day—they would open their eyes, look at the harvest, and begin readily reaping the other individuals the Kingdom's eye was upon. That, no matter their particular human skill set—most of that doesn't really matter anyway—they would draw their provisionary wage from Heaven itself and get down to harvesting. That, whether they felt their highest purpose to be in the planting, watering, tending or, again, reaping, they would be infinitely glad that their life had a heavenly purpose. That, even if they'd never done a lick of work in the preparation of another individual's heart—now ready for salvation—they'd manfully, woman-fully, reap the benefit of some other's past labor.

* * *

My friend, our original "certain individual" is *you*. Yours is the life I've been talking about, all along. You are the person with the particular backstory that matters most when it's drawn into the arc of the timeless exploits of that wonderful Man, Jesus of Nazareth. Your past life was interesting—to a degree. The particularities of your former way of life matter—to a point. But what's really, truly interesting about you, what will matter most at the end of your days, is how this period of following Jesus has gone. How you have answered the call to listen for His voice. How you have looked, each day, for practical ways to obey Him. How you have taken on His Spirit in ever greater measure. How faithful you have been, as someone who's been graced with the gospel yourself, to turn around—daily—and do something real with the ramifications of the gospel.

Let me put this positively:

Right now, there are certain other individuals walking on the face of the earth—men, women, and children—who are ripe with readiness for the realities of Jesus. Their individual backstories—the way they were raised, their outlook on the world, their hobbies and interests—perfectly suit them to hear His name from someone exactly like you. Yes, someone else has come before you: someone else has done the "hard work" to ensure that this man, woman, or child is ready to receive the gospel. So it is your *literal only job* to be awake enough, aware enough, present enough—*today*—to harvest this person for the Kingdom of God. You are the one who's meant to do it.

As far as you know, there's no one else. The barista at the coffee shop, the guy who cuts you off in traffic, your old college buddy, the worst woman you can't stand at your office, a homeless man on the sidewalk, a complete stranger who accosts you, someone you've been actively praying would meet Jesus for years—well, they're all waiting...for *you*.

You are the answer of Heaven for them.

You are the exact eyes and ears, and hands and feet, of Jesus.

The particularities of your whole human life—past, present, and future possibility—might hinge on your readiness to be a reaper in the harvest of the Kingdom of Heaven—*today*.

Isn't that exciting?

Section Two

HE NEVER FORGETS US

Promise
8

"For a brief moment I deserted you, but with great compassion I will gather you. In overflowing anger for a moment I hid my face from you, but with everlasting love I will have compassion on you,' says the Lord, your Redeemer. 'This is like the days of Noah to me: as I swore that the waters of Noah should no more go over the earth, so I have sworn that I will not be angry with you, and will not rebuke you. For the mountains may depart and the hills be removed, but my steadfast love shall not depart from you, and my covenant of peace shall not be removed,' says the Lord, who has compassion on you."

Isaiah 54:7-10 ESV

Until today, I had never read this promise in the way I'm now starting to read it—this morning I had a revelation about it that, I think, has forever changed its meaning for me. Before, I would've probably explained the idea of God's desertion and *"overflowing anger"* in the context of the Old Covenant and then ushered you right into a joyous reminder of the New. But that's what hit me this morning—the arrival of the New. The manner in which the New actually replaced the Old.

What if we read these words as words spoken not by God to the flailing Israelites—but as the words of the Father to the Son on the day of the Cross?

Consider:

"For a brief moment I deserted You,"—turned My eyes from Your sin-mantled Self, forsook You as You took on all mankind's transgressions to set them free—*"but with great compassion I will gather You.* I will raise You from the dead, My Son; You will stride from the tomb in Our shared victory.

"In overflowing anger for a moment I hid My face from You,"—and I know You felt it, Yeshua, and I know that it broke Your heart—*"but with everlasting love I will have compassion on You,"* Oh, how I will delight when You return to share this very throne with Me in only forty-three days!—*says the Lord, Your Redeemer*—Your Father, Your very shared Self.

"This is like the days of Noah to Me: as I swore that the waters of Noah should no more go over the earth, so I have sworn that I will not be angry with You, and will not rebuke You. Really, all human history will now be "the days of Jesus" to Me: as I swore that judgment would be pronounced on Him on behalf of all the earth, so I have sworn that any who abide in Him will also be set free from My rebuke.

"For the mountains may depart and the hills be removed,"—the very end of days may actually arrive—*"but My steadfast love shall not depart from You"*—for You are My Son, My Beloved, in whom My heart is forever pleased—*"and My covenant of peace shall not be removed,"*—not from You, not from the disciples of Your heart, nor from anyone who learns to call on Your name—*"says the Lord, who has compassion on You"*—and who

deeply loves You and loves Your obedience, even unto death, to set the world free.

What's making me a little emotional about that rendering of those words is that I've never fully focused—in that exchange—on the Father's breaking heart for His Son. Both of them had understood everything that was meant to happen, had been agreed would properly take place, and yet the agony the Father must've felt! Was it for *His* Son to actually have to bear the sins of mankind; to wear every sin of every man, woman, and child of the earth? He was the God of Heaven, this Son of His! How could this ugliness, this indignity fall upon Him?

And then, as *perfect* God, to actually have to go through with redemption's plan—to have to see His Son as sin itself *and to turn away?* Imagine how that moment must've rent the Father's heart. Oh! And then, as *perfect* Father, to actually have to watch as sinful men continued their mockery, persecution, murder—to have to watch your Son expire in the brutality of sin's separation? It must've felt too much; nearly impossible.

And yet…

And yet!

As sons and daughters of God ourselves, as recipients of the full bounty of all that Jesus gained that day, who can rejoice more than us at the final victory His death and resurrection won! We will never have to walk in the broken way the Israelites walked; we will never experience the Law; we are the freest people we've ever met—or even heard of! You and I are sons and daughters of God now! We stand to inherit everything the Cross bought!

In fact, in that vein, and knowing that Jesus *already did everything that was necessary in Heaven and upon earth to set us free,* let us reconsider today's promise in its final meaning. This is how God might describe where you and I stand today:

"For a brief moment, on a single day, on a Cross outside Jerusalem, I, your God, turned My back upon Myself, and with great compassion gathered you into My arms forever. In overflowing mercy for you, for a moment I laid My wrath upon My own Son, and with everlasting love I am now forever having compassion on you," says the Lord, our Redeemer, our Savior, the actual God who made us and who, by dying, re-made us.

"This is now the days of My Son and My Spirit: as He promised that the living waters of His Spirit would go over the earth, so I have agreed that those living waters should spring up from within you, and, in that way, that you would share Our very life. So the mountains and the hills may now be moved by faith as small as a mustard seed, and My steadfast love will be steadfast in your midst, never to depart. And My covenant of peace—the New Covenant, a covenant sworn between My Son and Me—will never be removed," says the Lord, our Father God, who has forever had compassion on us.

My friend, isn't the love of our God overwhelming? Let's go live an overwhelmed sort of day today.

Promise
9

"I, even I, am he who comforts you. Who are you that you fear mere mortals, human beings who are but grass, that you forget the Lord your Maker, who stretches out the heavens and who lays the foundations of the earth, that you live in constant terror every day because of the wrath of the oppressor, who is bent on destruction? For where is the wrath of the oppressor? The cowering prisoners will soon be set free; they will not die in their dungeon, nor will they lack bread. For I am the Lord your God, who stirs up the sea so that its waves roar—the Lord Almighty is his name. I have put my words in your mouth and covered you with the shadow of my hand...."

ISAIAH 51:12-16 NIV

As you listen to the push and pull of this promise—the way God speaks of His faithfulness, our fear, His "ever-presentness"—it begins to rise from the page that the entirety of this promise can be summed up in three words: **Position, Forgetfulness, Remembrance.** Both He and we are specifically *positioned*, in Heaven and on earth, in precisely the ways He's ordained so that His goodness attains its proper glory. However, our *forgetfulness* often gets in the way of our acceptance and enjoyment of our position—we undercut the heavenly value proposition that He has richly provided. But, remembering, being reminded, coming into a surety founded upon *remembrance*, we're suddenly lifted right back into our proper position before Him—with Him. This promise is a timely reminder that the only snares separating our heavenly inheritance from our earthly experience are these incursions of our fleshly forgetfulness.

Let's stop forgetting today, shall we?

First off, the words He speaks to our **Position**:

"I, even I, am he who comforts you." Our only comfort is to be found in Him. In God. In the Father, the Son, and the Holy Spirit. On any given day, you may stop whatever you're doing, sit perfectly still wherever you are, and actually ask to be internally comforted. He will comfort you, right there and then.

"The cowering prisoners will soon be set free…" Or, better yet: The cowering prisoners *have been* set free! You are already free—*today!* The blood of Jesus has already warranted for your perfect, holy blamelessness; you cannot be more free than you already are. He has promised that—and then done the entire work to make it so.

"They will not die in their dungeon…" Your circumstances today are not the whole story. No matter what you're presently experiencing, no matter the hardships you're currently enduring, you are not outside of how He would seek to lead and care for you. Can you, today, trust Him? He will not allow you to languish unnecessarily. He is actually working out something in your life, right this minute.

"Nor will they lack bread." He is the only Provider you've ever had. Your paycheck isn't the boss of you. Your boss isn't the boss of you. The One who easily feeds the birds of the air and clothes the grass of the fields isn't without resources that specifically have your name on them. Will you trust Him—and ask?

"I have put my words in your mouth..." Jesus promised His disciples that whenever they were dragged before governors and kings for His sake, He would literally speak His words right from their mouths. Again, here, it's promised: He will arm you with proper words. He wants His sons and daughters to always have the Holy Spirit-infused vocabulary for every situation: He has promised it.

"And covered you with the shadow of my hand..." Your life lives in the shadow—not of death, or discouragement, nor of sin, or of hopelessness, or despair—but in the cool, fresh shade of His mighty hand. Nothing can get to you that doesn't have His allowance for your good. No arrow or word or trial can ever outflank Him. You are presently nested right within His will, under the awe-inspiringly, massive power of His hand; you are right where you belong. Your position is assured. You are beloved. You are His.

Yet, tragically, we often forget everything I just wrote. We ignore our position. We lapse into a **Forgetfulness** that precludes enjoyment of our position.

"Who are you that you fear mere mortals, human beings who are but grass, that you forget the Lord your Maker, who stretches out the heavens and who lays the foundations of the earth..." One would think that being intimately involved with our Maker—our

literal Designer, Tinkerer, Creator—who literally stretched the heavens across the arc of the earth, who dropped the plumb line and created the foundations upon which everything is built, would always overawe our human sensibilities. And we might think that knowing the One who personally came to ensure our heavenward arrival, who went to a Cross to set us free from sin and satan, who conquered death so that we too might conquer death, might ever and always have our full attention. In that case, we would be wrong. Absolutely, sadly, amazingly. In a word, our perfect, heavenly position gets undercut most by our ability to focus our full attention on our fellow man. We live in fear of man and forget our God. What a foolishly underwhelming exchange of attention!

"[Who are you] that you live in constant terror every day because of the wrath of the oppressor, who is bent on destruction?" This is a particularly silly act of personal forgetfulness! Because—don't forget!—the "oppressor, who is bent on destruction" has been defeated, once and for all time, by the final act of Jesus at the Cross of Calvary! The enemy has been outwitted, out-marched, outclassed, out-armed and has been shamed by the perfect, heavenly outcome achieved by Jesus. We have nothing to fear from his direction, the enemy is defeated.

Which brings us to the wonderful opportunity we have for daily, personal **Remembrance** of all we hold in knowing our God personally.

Look:

"For where is the wrath of the oppressor?" Everything I just wrote is everything He always wants you remembering, all the time, every minute of every day. Or, even better, as Paul said it:

*Christ has completely abolished death, and has now,
through the Gospel, opened to us men the shining pos-
sibilities of the life that is eternal* (2 Timothy 1:10
PNT).

Jesus didn't only rob the evil one of his wrath and power
to cause us guilt and shame, Jesus gave us an infinite inheritance to hold in satan's face. Wrath is replaced by glory; hate
by heavenly love; fear by confidence founded on the Founder
of All Things.

*"For I am the Lord your God, who stirs up the sea so that
its waves roar—the Lord Almighty is his name."* Your faithful
Friend, the One who has already done everything to ensure
the quality of His every promise, is the Lord your God, the
God of the universe. His fingertip stirs the sea so that its
waves roar. His voice in the night can also calm the waves.
The Lord Almighty is His name—His name is also Jesus of
Nazareth: the One whose Gospel is the living Way that He
personally personifies.

Shall we spend today *remembering* all of this?

Promise
10

"Two sparrows sell for a farthing, don't they? Yet not a single sparrow falls to the ground without your Father's knowledge. The very hairs of your head are all numbered. Never be afraid, then—you are far more valuable than sparrows."

MATTHEW 10:29-31 PHILLIPS

The way you just read those words is the way those three verses actually read. Now let me narrate the way we usually, actually read them for ourselves:

"Two sparrows sell for a farthing, don't they?"

Yes, Jesus, they do. Sparrows are very cheap. (Although it's been many moons since I bought a sparrow at market.) And, by the way, I already know what you're going to say in the next couple sentences, Jesus. I know this is a parable of sorts. And, of course, I'll read and listen as closely as I can. But, naturally, I'm not a sparrow and I have all kinds of others things on my mind today. And even though I know You're very loving, and that You have my best interests at heart, I also know that the day is going to absolutely fly by. Pun not intended. But lots of things to get done, Jesus. Lots of items on my list...

Anyhow, what were You saying?

"Yet not a single sparrow falls to the ground without your Father's knowledge."

Which is very nice for the sparrows, I'm sure, Jesus. But here's two things I've got to bring up, right away. A sparrow falling to the ground, known or not, has already fallen to the ground. I'm not sure I'm comforted by that. After all, falling to the ground, I'd prefer *not* falling to the ground. I'd prefer a little warning about my life; to know if I'm slated to possibly fall to the ground—today or tomorrow or whenever. Is that something we could talk about, Jesus?

And the second thing: I've never really known much about the Father. He feels very mysterious to me. I think I've got a pretty good idea of what *You're* up to, Jesus—but the Father? I don't know. His knowledge of me feels about as nebulous as my knowledge of Him. He's watching out for all the sparrows—not letting them fall to the ground, and all that—but what about *me*? How am I supposed to be known by the One I hardly know? Is this parable specifically about *me*?

"The very hairs of your head are all numbered."

Great. Now that's something. But I'm hearing You mixing your metaphor, Jesus, going from the sparrows to my head of hair, and I'm wondering how that particular knowledge will particularly help me? I grant that's a pretty unbelievable show of mathematic mindedness, though! I have a pretty nice crop of hair up there...

What are You looking at, Jesus? *Jesus?*

"Never be afraid, then—"

And I'll cut you off, right there. *Never be afraid?* Never being afraid is one of those commands that feels almost ridiculous, Jesus, when I look at the context of the modern world. Let me help You understand my daily worries. I wake up fairly fearful about the way the day will go. I already know I'm behind on three separate projects at work. Brushing my teeth, I'm also already worried about the next batch of bills soon to present themselves. Then, driving to work, I'm back to fearing how our eventual merger with another company might adversely affect my standing within my group. And, all day, I move from worry to worry to worry.

And that's without my fears for our kids. One of them is fine; the other, not so much. And now we're into our next season of sports and I'm pretty concerned that neither is tracking with the rest of the kids on their team and then how will they ever get playing time in high school? And what about getting a scholarship for college?

Which brings up college. *What about college, Jesus?* Do You have any idea what that costs these days? Do You think I have a snowball's chance of ever scraping up enough to handle even the *possibility* of even a state-school for either of them?

Do you see what I mean here, Jesus? About that *"Never be afraid"* as a point of practicality? I'm up to my ears in fear and You're coming to me with sparrows, falling, the Father, my hair, and telling me to never be *afraid?*

And what was that last thing You always say here?

"You are far more valuable than sparrows."

Ah, yes. Sparrows again. I had a feeling the sparrows would make their reappearance. So, the sparrows—being awfully cheap at market—occasionally falling, but within the Father's knowledge, are much less valuable than me? That's what You're saying here?

Do You have anything else You'd like to share with me, Jesus?

* * *

Does that sound anything like the wandering, arguing, scattered state of mind you personally experience when you're reading through the Scriptures some days? That what you're reading through gets qualified against the reality of that morning—or that week of work—and then descends to your spirit in chaos? That the simplicity of the parables and portraitures of Jesus gets somehow lost amid the swirling onrush of your day ahead?

I promise you, you're not alone in that. You're not the only one whose time in the Word gets muddled. It happens to every single one of us. My little argument with Jesus, where I had us going back and forth with His words, was maybe the easiest thing I've written all year. Because it's easy to harvest the words of doubt and unbelief. A skeptic's voice is almost our most native tongue, these days. And it's somehow easier for us to guard our minds with half-belief in His promises than to reckon with the weight of simply, fully trusting Him: believing.

Today, I'd like to simply, fully believe in Jesus. And I'd like you to join me in that.

Jesus says: *"Two sparrows sell for a farthing, don't they?"* Yes. Sparrows are insignificant in almost everyone's eyes.

"Yet not a single sparrow falls to the ground without your Father's knowledge." Meaning that the Father does not miss a thing. His nature is a perfect knowledge of everything. His grasp of detail is absolutely infinite. There is nothing in my day today, your day today, that will elude His understanding or His perfect care for me or you. And if you don't know the Father well for yourself, you can immediately turn your gaze on Jesus. The Father and He are one. Coming to Jesus, you have arrived to the Father.

"The very hairs of your head are all numbered." The God of Heaven sees you. He is with you right now. And He's delighted with what He sees of you. And He absolutely loves you. In fact, before you were born, before your parents or grandparents or family line were born, He was already absolutely enraptured at the very thought of you. He loved you so much, in fact, that knowing of your predicament as a fallen child of Adam and Eve, He personally died to set you free. He sees you. He knows you. He loves you.

"Never be afraid, then—" Because, why would you? Why should you ever be afraid again? *"...If God is for us, who can be against us? He that did not hesitate to spare his own Son but gave him up for us all—can we not trust such a God to give us, with him, everything else that we can need?"* (Romans 8:31-32 Phillips). There is nothing in the heavens or the earth that can touch you when the sparrow-watching, hair-counting Father of us all is the Father of *you*. The God of Heaven is your Father-God.

Your Savior—and your heavenly Brother—is Jesus. Never. Be. Afraid. Then.

"You are far more valuable than sparrows." Whom, by the way, He loves.

I would wager that our lives feel filled with intolerable complexity, too often, because we've tolerated too much unbelief, too long. Today, let's be different. Let's believe. Let's let promises like these lead the way, all day.

Our God knows everything. He sees you perfectly—and perfected. He loves you to the end of Himself.

Let's live fearlessly in that reality.

It's the only reality there actually is.

Promise
11

"But Zion said, 'The Lord has forsaken me, the Lord has forgotten me.' Can a mother forget the baby at her breast and have no compassion on the child she has borne? Though she may forget, I will not forget you! See, I have engraved you on the palms of my hands...."

Isaiah 49:14-16 NIV

Imagine the feeling of feeling totally left out, not part of the crowd, on the outside of the greatest happening that ever happened in human history. Imagine all the feelings of bewilderment, incredulousness, annoyance, uncertainty, and doubt as you watched and witnessed everyone else's excitement. They are positively brimming with joy—eyes alight, holding each other by the shoulders and shaking each other, shouting, "Can you believe it?!" As the evening wears on, their group stupefaction loses none of its luster; they only smile the wider as their realization takes deeper root.

They have all seen Jesus—resurrected.

You are Thomas—you didn't.

The next few days are certainly among the worst days you've ever lived through: their awe and delight grates upon you like nothing else. Each morning, all the apostles and disciples spring from their beds, watching the door, waiting for another heavenly incursion of the alive-again, smiling, peace-bringing Savior.

Your own position becomes more and more entrenched.

"Unless I see Him for myself, I'll never believe," you keep telling them.

Of course, in the back of your mind and heart, you are all along hoping that the whole thing is real: that Jesus is actually alive and readily re-available. It wasn't too long before this week—the journey, in fact, when Lazarus was raised from the dead—when you'd been perfectly willing to die with Him. You love Jesus. You've treasured every minute with Him. There could be nothing finer than to see Him again.

But the persistent sense of missing His reappearance, of not being part of that group experience together, haunts your heart. You are hurt you missed the moment—and you can't shake it. No one else's word will suffice for personal experience.

And that's precisely the thought you're thinking, sitting in the upper room, a few nights later, when you casually look up and—

There He is!

Jesus is standing on the other end of the room—just past the others, who haven't noticed Him yet—and He's staring steadily at you. He is cloaked in a bright white coat of the richest, thickest material; He is standing squared-off, straight, shoulders aimed right at you. In a moment, He will smile that familiar, wonderful smile…right now, He is not smiling. His eyes are afire with power. His brow is heavy. The way His face and carriage incline themselves toward you, the look in His eyes, almost shout across the room—and here's what they say:

"You seem to think, Thomas, 'The Lord has forsaken me, the Lord has forgotten me.' Thomas! Can a mother forget the baby at her breast and have no compassion on the child she has borne? Though she may forget, I will not forget you! See?"

He raises His hands, holding the palms toward you, for your viewing—*"I have engraved you on the palms of my hands…."*

* * *

Like Thomas, have you ever felt that feeling of feeling left out, not part of the crowd, on the outside of the unconquerable fellowship of those who have really experienced Jesus? Have you ever felt bewilderment, incredulousness, annoyance, uncertainty, or doubt while you watched and witnessed everyone else's excitement? Those worship services positively brimming with joy? Followers of Jesus with eyes constantly alight? The way they hold each other by the shoulders, shaking each other, shouting in each other's faces, *"Can you believe this?!"*? How week after week rolls by and their joy and satisfaction seems to lose none of its luster; how they smile the wider as their realization seems to take deeper root?

They claim to have experienced Jesus—contemporaneously alive.

To you—you've just been going through the motions.

All the Sunday mornings and worship nights and Bible studies can sometimes feel like the worst: everyone's awe and delight grate upon you like nothing else. Sometimes it feels like all the others simply get out of bed, crack open their Bible, and have immediate interchange with the alive, smiling, peace-bringing Savior.

So, your own position has become more and more entrenched.

"Unless I feel it for myself, I'll never believe," you keep saying.

Of course, in the back of your mind and heart, you are all along hoping that the whole thing is real: that Jesus is totally alive and readily re-available. It wasn't so long ago—it seems almost like yesterday when you cast your mind back—that you'd been perfectly willing to do anything in the whole wide world He might've asked. You absolutely love Jesus of Nazareth. You treasure every little bit of revelation He's given of Himself. There could be nothing finer than experiencing more of His presence.

But the persistent sense of not enjoying everything everyone else is enjoying, of not being part of those Holy Spirit happenings, haunts your heart. You feel hurt you've missed some instances of His presence—and you can't shake it. No one else's word will suffice for personal experience.

And perhaps that's the precise thought you're thinking, sitting wherever you are, right now, when actually it's your whole heavenly duty to remember—

Here He is!

He is alive in the room you're in—alive in Heaven—alive in you—and His eyes are steadily upon you. He is robed in the richest cloak of the Prince of Peace; He is seated upon the throne of Heaven, totally focused on you. In a moment, He'll be smiling that familiar, wonderful smile—right now, He is not smiling. His eyes are afire with power. His brow is heavy. The way His face and carriage incline themselves toward you, the way He leans forward, almost shouts across the heavens— and here's what they say:

"You seem to think, 'The Lord has forsaken me, the Lord has forgotten me.' My beloved! Can a mother forget the baby at her breast and have no compassion on the child she has borne? Though she may forget, I will not forget you! See?"

—He raises both His hands, holding the palms toward you, so you can see—

"I have engraved you on the palms of my hands..."

And now, as He said to Thomas on that night in the upper room, He is saying to you: "Stop doubting—and believe."

THE JOY OF TURNING TO HIM

Promise
12

"I tell you, there will be more joy in heaven over one sinner who repents than over ninety-nine righteous persons who need no repentance"

Luke 15:7 ESV

Here, again, we're hearing of another of the radical differences between the mechanics of the Old and New Covenants: in the Old, the only celebrated class of individual would be the perfectly religiously righteous; in the New, the party erupts over one real, repentant sinner. The difference—and its practical ramifications for us—cannot be overstated.

Under the Old Covenant, *every single action* within your day today would've required mindfulness—not so much toward positive action, or helping others, or living joyfully and hopefully—but simply not in breaking the Law *at all*. Every moment, from your waking to your sleeping, you would've been on pins and needles, balancing hundreds of requirements in your head, scores of ancient dos and don'ts. Then, of course, naturally, being human, you'd blow it.

So, whether today or tomorrow or on a predetermined day of the week that you typically preferred, it'd be over to the tabernacle or temple for some ritual, religious slaughter. You'd pay the fee for the animal—or bring your own—and then you'd watch as a priest went through the ceremony of slitting its throat, spilling its blood, proclaiming your sin upon it: all of that. Then you were free—for a time. Because in leaving the temple or tabernacle and walking back out through the gate into the real world, you were still perfectly human, perfectly fallible, perfectly on your own in this.

In fact, that's it—the tragedy of the Old Covenant, the reason it didn't and couldn't work, is that the individual stayed totally individualized. The Old Covenant was always a party of one.

Now let's look at the New Covenant:

> *After this, Jesus went out and saw a tax collector by the name of Levi sitting at his tax booth. "Follow me," Jesus said to him, and Levi got up, left everything and followed him. Then Levi held a great banquet for Jesus at his house, and a large crowd of tax collectors and others were eating with them. But the Pharisees and the teachers of the law who belonged to their sect complained to his disciples, "Why do you eat and drink with tax collectors and sinners?" Jesus answered them, "It is not the healthy who need a doctor, but the sick. I have not come to call the righteous, but sinners to repentance"* (Luke 5:27-32 NIV).

In Mark's rendering of this moment, one of my favorite details also gets added into the opening of this party at Levi's villa. After introducing the partygoers—tax-collectors and disreputable folk—Mark's account casually mentions: *"For there were **many such people** among his followers"* (Mark 2:15 Phillips).

Under the New Covenant, disreputable people are constantly, instantly drawn to the presence of Jesus, where they repent, follow Him, and instantly, constantly throw parties of salvation. You see, the *"joy in heaven over one sinner who repents"* is actually communicable: it transmits straight from Jesus into the repentant heart—freeing it and teaching it the new way to party. How to turn right around and hold a great banquet, like Levi. How to invite a large crowd of tax collectors and other sinners. How to properly mix and mingle with the other disreputable folk already around. How to rightly rouse some rabble with the newly righteous, now-repentant rest of this rabble around Jesus.

In fact, for any branch of the Church, any denomination, any church, any fellowship, any Bible Study, any accountability group, any Christian individual, I'd ask you: Are these sorts of great banquets of salvation breaking out within your midst? Are you constantly seeing this *"joy in heaven"* happening within your four walls? Do "disreputable folk" have the habit of gravitating to what you're doing, finding repentance readily, following Jesus, and joining the party?

If yes, well done!

If no, I can almost guarantee why…

- What you're doing doesn't resemble a party.
- Levi's banquet is the furthest thing from your worship service.

▪ Jesus is, ostensibly, the center of what you're up to, but His personal joy in meeting sinners isn't.

If you and I—if congregations and councils and pastors and popes—want to enjoy the fruits of the New Covenant, then *we must enjoy the New Covenant!* We must ourselves repent daily—setting off little re-runs of our own original, heavenly salvation-party—and then we must get down to the actual business of following Jesus. We must weave in and out of all the city streets and squares with Him. We must proceed with Him right into the halls of our work or school. We must re-train our eyes to see the sorts of people we *used* to be—disreputable folk—and recognize the "sick" who need our perfect "Doctor."

And, seeing them, what are we to do next?

What sort of conclave are we inviting them into?

An Old Covenant form of solo, sacrificial, grinding, methodical über-mindfulness?

Or the New Covenant of Heaven? The joyous, personal, repentant, inviting, **now**, happening, open, full, *still* joyous, centered-around-the-living-presence-of-Jesus Living Way?

Today, let's hold out the promise of today's promise. Let's throw the New Covenant party people are actually dying for. All we have to do is point them to or back to Jesus. He is both the Doctor for the sick—and the true Life of the party.

Promise

13

"If My people who are called by My name will humble themselves, and pray and seek My face, and turn from their wicked ways, then I will hear from heaven, and will forgive their sin and heal their land. Now My eyes will be open and My ears attentive to prayer made in this place"

2 Chronicles 7:14-15 NKJV

How great would it be to wake up knowing that the loving eyes of God were upon you; that His ears were pricked up and attentive to your every need, your every prayer, your every whisper; that His hearing you from Heaven would instantly unleash full forgiveness of sin, healing for yourself and for all the others around you? Wouldn't that be wonderful? Also, wouldn't it be so powerful to point all people to a God like that—a God so rich in mercy and attentive to His sons and daughters? Wouldn't our worldwide Great Commission dreams of seeing all nations encountering Him be accomplished all the more readily if *we ourselves* so encountered Him?

Then, simply, as this promise so blatantly states, we need only *humble ourselves, pray, seek His face,* and *turn from our wicked ways.* That's it. That's all. That and only that. After which, everything I just stated in that first paragraph becomes our reality: His hearing, forgiveness, healing, open eyes and ears become our natural atmosphere of life and living. In other words, if we would see the world see Jesus, if we would want to carry out the Master Plan, we need only heed the pointed words of these verses.

But doesn't everything I just said sound oddly religious? Like a litany of inward self-corrections and self-amendments? When you read my language of "just do this" or "just do that," isn't there a little part of you that knows you're absolutely destined to fail?

So, instead, let's be reminded of the *context* of these words—when the Lord first spoke them to a human listener—and then we'll reframe our plan for encountering the glories of this promise.

Here's the end of 2 Chronicles 6 and the opening of 7. King Solomon is praying in his newly built Temple:

> *"Now, my God, I pray, let Your eyes be open and let Your ears be attentive to the prayer made in this place. 'Now therefore, arise, O Lord God, to Your resting place, You and the ark of Your strength. Let Your priests, O Lord God, be clothed with salvation, and let Your saints rejoice in goodness. O Lord God, do not turn away the face of Your Anointed; remember the mercies of Your servant David."*
>
> *When Solomon had finished praying, fire came down from heaven and consumed the burnt offering and the*

sacrifices; and the glory of the Lord filled the temple. And the priests could not enter the house of the Lord, because the glory of the Lord had filled the Lord's house. When all the children of Israel saw how the fire came down, and the glory of the Lord on the temple, they bowed their faces to the ground on the pavement, and worshiped and praised the Lord, saying: "For He is good, for His mercy endures forever" (2 Chronicles 6:40-7:3 NKJV).

When you read a promise like today's promise—with its seeming list of required, inward self-helps—there's a temptation to buckle down, do the work, become the best version of your worshipping self, and expect to see the reward for your satisfactory religiosity. If only you would be humble—then He would hear. *If only* you would properly pray—then He would forgive you. *If only* you would seek His face—then He'd heal. *If only* you would stop that wickedness—then He'd open His eyes and ears.

But that way of reading today's promise *totally forgets* the actual reality in which these words were spoken to King Solomon—in eyeshot of the glory-cloud of God's presence hanging above the Temple He'd filled with Himself! And did you notice the people's natural reaction? Down-on-their-faces personal humility. Did you notice the people's first action? Worship and praise in the form of prayer. Did you hear how they first praised Him? With words that proclaimed the glory of His face. Do you get a sense of their next steps? Now, in His presence, to turn away from wickedness.

If you desire to have your prayers heard, full forgiveness, healing all around you, to feel the eyes of God upon you, His ears attentive to your every word, then you have one of two options:

1. You can muscle out the qualifiers for this promise from your own limited human strength.

Or:

2. You can reside in His glory. You can rest. You can let Him do it.

The most humble, prayerful, seeing-the-face-of-God, turned-totally-from-all-wicked-ways people are the ones who've relentlessly placed their lives in the path of His glory. They have experienced Jesus, never turned away from experiencing Jesus, and, today, only want to experience Jesus more. They have tasted the glory of the Holy Spirit, asked for more of the Holy Spirit, and, today, are asking for ever more of the Holy Spirit. They are obsessed with the glory of God. They can never get enough of the Presence.

Because, having tasted, having seen that the Lord is good and gracious and wildly extravagant with His glory—they want it. They want nothing more, and nothing less, than everything He's willing to give them of Himself—they want it all.

Because, seeing their inner lives all filled with that same glory Solomon once saw, they find that nothing now separates their lives from the life of Jesus. *His* humility, *His* way of praying, *His* seeking of the Father, *His* purity have become the natural way of their human lives. They are walking with Jesus—*now*. They are beginning to walk like Jesus—*today*.

So, what do you think? Should we spend today bootstrapping our way toward obedience—or should we get in the glory and truly live? Should we "try our best" and maybe only achieve our best—or see all the best of what Jesus, by His Spirit, offers us?

The choice today is yours.

Promise 14

"...Return to me, says the Lord of hosts, and I will return to you, says the Lord of hosts."

Zechariah 1:3 ESV

A trio of questions for your consideration:

1. How does the God who never leaves us, ever return to us?

2. How does the God who never turns away, ever turn back?

3. How does the One whose presence immanently, spatially, spiritually covers the earth and heavens, seem to reappear?

Answers:

1. We *perceive* His presence once again.

2. We, *being attuned,* lock eyes with Him.

3. By *focusing* our limited, individual, bodily, fleshly selves through the lens of His Spirit—who is One with Himself and yet within us—we link our human lives to God Himself.

So, it is *perception, attunement,* and *Holy Spirit-focus* that unlocks the glory of today's promise for today's experience. It is for us to take some simple steps to enjoy His ever-present presence, to look in His direction, to commune with Him by His very own Spirit.

Shall we, together, take those steps today?

I say, Let's!

In a moment, we'll be making our way through five separate parts of our human life, returning to Him with confession, gratitude, worship, thanksgiving—whatever it means to you, today, to so **return to Him**. First, you'll read a list of ways He's personally blessed you in each area of life and then—wherever you are—I'd ask that you take a moment, take a deep breath, and return to Him in that part of your life. Again, it may be confession that's needed, there. Or, reading what you read, you might break out in spontaneous gratitude and worship.

But what's important is that, believing this promise, desiring experience of His presence, we bring our *focus, attunement,* and *perceptiveness* to the reality of His being beside us, within us, always with us.

Here you go—feel free to use the blank spaces for recording your prayers and thoughts:

At the level of your basic, daily needs—food, water, health, provision—what do you want to say to Him? How does your heart move in returning to Him, there?

Next: When you think of how He's protected you, how He's kept you safe and taken care of you, how He's guided your life into places of true life, how would you voice your returning?

_____

_____

_____

How about the people He's placed in your life? How about family? Friends? Coworkers? What about the way He's masterfully woven relationships into the fabric of your story? Return to Him in that part of your life.

_____

_____

_____

And when you think of how He chose you—how He turned in the midst of the crowd of all humanity, saw you, pointed, and said, "That one! That one is Mine"? What do you want to say to Him in His love for you? How have you experienced that expression of His choice of you? Return to Him in that wonderful place.

_____

_____

_____

And, last: Do you know that He lived for you, died for you, rose for you, ascended for you, sent His Holy Spirit to you? How do you want to return to Him when you know that He's already done everything to ensure that you can return to Him? How do you respond to His every glorious salvation action?

———————————————————————————————

———————————————————————————————

My friend, isn't it truly lovely that in the space of a very few minutes, we have had opportunity to *perceive, attune,* and *focus*—by Himself—upon Himself? Isn't it wondrous that on every day of our little human lives we can actually link those lives to the very One who is Life?

———————————————————————————————

———————————————————————————————

Last question: How has He returned to *you* today? What have you experienced of *Him*?

———————————————————————————————

———————————————————————————————

Perhaps take a few moments to ponder and close out this time by recording anything specific you've received from Him:

———————————————————————————————

———————————————————————————————

———————————————————————————————

Promise
15

"For I know the plans I have for you, declares the Lord, plans to prosper you and not to harm you, to give you a future and a hope. Then you will call upon Me and come and pray to Me, and I will listen to you. You will seek Me and find Me when you search for Me with all your heart"

JEREMIAH 29:11-13 BSB

Picture yourself standing in the hot, direct sunlight of the high desert; the only wind blowing in your direction, even hotter still. Below you, down the bank, are gliding the greenish-gray waters of the Jordan River, and yet its coolness makes no impact upon the afternoon's heat. You are standing just a few feet away from a small group of people at the edge of a much larger crowd of people: you are one of John the Baptist's disciples. He has finished his work of ministry for the day—no more teaching or time in the river—and you are wondering what the late-afternoon and evening will hold.

Suddenly you hear John's voice, "Behold! The Lamb of God!"

You follow his hand in the direction he's pointing and see, just at the far fringe of the crowd, a Man walking off in the opposite direction. His head and shoulders and back look just like everyone else's—nothing betrays any hint of grandeur in His clothing, sandals, walk, or the way He swings His arms.

You look back at your teacher, John.

He nods his head to you: *Go.*

So, you and another disciple of John wind your way along the edge of the crowd, heading northward, following that solitary Figure along and up the dusty road. He walks surprisingly swiftly. His gait is long and straight and undiminished by the afternoon's heat—it is difficult to keep up as He approaches the hills. The light is starting to drop when you finally get closer. You are surrounded, now, by the low trees and bushes of the foothills.

Then, stopping, the Man casts a glance over His shoulder.

He studies your pair of faces for a moment.

"What do you want?" He asks. Just that. *What do you want?*

He might've asked it as, "*What* do you want?" or "What do *you* want?" where the obvious emphasis would've implied that your presence was undesirable, undesired. Instead, it was "What do you *want?*"—and spoken in a manner to imply that, upon hearing your desire, He could actually do something demonstrative about that desire.

You hear your own voice speak up, "Teacher, where are You abiding?"

He smiles. He points up the way. "Come and see."

* * *

The next morning, after a delightful dinner, an overwhelmingly wonderful twilight conversation, a good night's sleep under the spreading shade of a fig tree, you awake. And there He is: Jesus, the Man from Nazareth. He has just, Himself, awoken. He is rising to His feet to see about some breakfast for the three of you.

"And what will we do today, Jesus?" you ask Him. "What are Your plans?"

He smiles again. "Come and see."

Day after day after day: "Come and see."

Come, He says.

And see.

* * *

"For I know the plans I have for you, declares the Lord, plans to prosper you and not to harm you, to give you a future and a hope. Then you will call upon Me and come and pray to Me, and I will listen to you. You will seek Me and find Me when you search for Me with all your heart."

My friend, the glory and awe of following the Way of Jesus is that the Way of Jesus is the Man those disciples caught up with in John 1. We are not walking along some strange, esoteric, philosophically religious moral pathway that ends in some puzzling form of heightened self-actualization. We are following Jesus, the Man from Nazareth.

And, seeking Him, searching for Him, finding Him ever more with more of our heart, we may come to Him and call to Him, praying to One who listens. For He literally already knows the plans He has for us: Kingdom-of-Heaven strategies to prosper and grow and grant us eternity's everlasting hope.

The Man who quietly turned His head on the road out of that wilderness is the very same One who turns His head today and asks you: "What do you *want*?"

My question is: What do you want?

Do you want to know for yourself where He abides?

In you!

Do you want to know what He has for your future?

"Come and see."

Do you want to know exactly what you should do today?

"Come and see."

Come, He still says, beckoning you ever nearer, every minute of every day—

And see.

Promise
16

"Behold, I stand at the door and knock; if anyone hears My voice and opens the door, I will come in to him and will dine with him, and he with Me."

What's most fascinating about the words of this well-known, oft-written-about promise aren't necessarily the words themselves, but instead the *hearers* who first heard them read aloud: the "lukewarm" church at Laodicea, one of the seven First-Century churches spoken to, by Jesus, in the Book of Revelation. Can you imagine sitting in the fellowship at Laodicea, receiving that miraculous, written-down revelation of Heaven from John, and then hearing that you were, more likely than not, on the cusp of being "spit out of [Jesus'] mouth"? (Revelation 3:16). That, even though you'd been week-by-weekly going through the motions of meeting, doing your nice little services, you'd been deluding yourselves about the reality of your obedience?

What a moment that must've been!

But even *more* remarkable is the fact that, after all the difficult words Jesus speaks to this wayward fellowship, He then turns right around and offers up today's promise to them. He changes the subject by saying, *"All those whom I love I correct and discipline. Therefore, shake off your complacency and repent"* (Revelation 3:19 PNT) and then speaks today's *"Behold…"*

How wonderful is Jesus! That no matter how we've lost our way, wandered from His Way, got into patterns of self-delusion, fruitless living, lukewarm folly—He always calls us back! He knocks at the door of our hearts and—if we'll only just crack the door, say, "Who's there?"—He'll walk right in and set the table for dinner together! This is the glorious God we belong to! This is the Savior with that beautiful salvation-smirk on His face!

Which leads me to my other favorite part of this promise in its Laodicean context, within in its broader "Seven Churches of Revelation" context. Did you know that, despite all the foibles and up-and-down obedience and disobedience of that group of churches, each word to each church ends in the very same way? It's true. Each church is spurred toward fresh faithfulness by a promise Jesus gives of what will happen to, and for, those who He calls *"the victorious."*

So in light of the promise of One who will walk right in and renew His love and personal fellowship with us, I'd like you to read all seven *"victorious"* statements for yourself. These are from Revelation 2 and 3, after each word to each church.

Here they are—with a short Eugene thought after each:

"To the victorious I will give the right to eat from the tree of life which grows in the paradise of God" (Revelation 2:7 Phillips).

The Jesus who'll knock at the door, allow you to answer, then come on in, set the table, sit down to eat, is the very same Jesus who will feast with you on fruit from the Tree of Life—*forever.*

"The victorious cannot suffer the slightest hurt from the second death" (Revelation 2:11 Phillips).

Death and the second death hold nothing that can ever hurt you. For you belong to Jesus, the almighty, eternal Victor.

I will give the victorious some of the hidden manna, and I will also give him a white stone with a new name written upon it which no man knows except the man who receives it (Revelation 2:17 Phillips).

He leans across the table and hands you some of His heavenly bread—*today and forever!*—and also a new name He's been hiding in His heart—*just for you.*

To the one who is victorious, who carries out my work to the end, I will give authority over the nations, just as I myself have received authority from my Father, and I will give him the morning star. "He shall rule them with a rod of iron; as the potter's vessels shall be broken to pieces" (Revelation 2:26-29 Phillips).

In His economy, you are gloriously mighty.

The victorious shall wear such white garments, and never will I erase his name from the book of life. Indeed, I will speak his name openly in the presence of my Father and of his angels (Revelation 3:5 Phillips).

Because of His perfect love, you are pure, holy, and blameless.

As for the victorious, I will make him a pillar in the Temple of my God, and he will never leave it. I will write upon him the name of my God, and the name of the city of my God, the new Jerusalem which comes down out of Heaven from my God. And I will write upon him my own new name (Revelation 3:12 Phillips).

Jesus, the One who would dine with you today—feeding you fruit from the Tree of Life and hidden, heavenly manna—is the God of Heaven. He is making you into a permanent pillar for His Temple; a known, named member of His mighty ones; one who personally shares in His name.

And then comes the amazing word spoken to the hearers of today's promise, the Laodicean fellowship:

> *As for the victorious, I will give him the honour of sitting beside me on my throne, just as I myself have won the victory and have taken my seat beside my Father on his throne* (Revelation 3:21 Phillips).

My friend, the Jesus who is knocking on your door today, wanting to take His meals at your table, is also the Jesus who will one day invite you up onto His throne! The One who has *made* you holy and blameless—fit for Heaven and victorious with His victory—is the One who can't wait to say to His Father, "Could You slide over a little? One of my best friends has finally arrived. This one who heard My knock, opened the door, let Me in, and dined with Me—is now here with us, Father. Slide on over. Let's let this one sit between us—*forever.*"

Thank You, Jesus.

Section Four

ANSWERED PRAYER

Promise
17

"Call to me and I will answer you and tell you great and unsearchable things you do not know."

JEREMIAH 33:3 NIV

On the day these words were uttered by the lips of God, here were realities of the earthly circumstances of His listeners:

- The Babylonian army was, right then, laying siege to the city of Jerusalem.

- The hearer, Jeremiah, was confined in the courtyard of the palace of the king, Zedekiah, who was a puppet king presently in rebellion against the ruler of Babylon, hence the siege.

- Within a few years:

    - The walls of Jerusalem would be entirely leveled.

    - The palace itself would be destroyed.

    - Solomon's Temple would be burnt to the ground.

- Only the poorest of the poor would be left to tend to the vineyards and fields of Judah.

- All the other people would be in exile in Babylon.

Yet with all of that real, and true, and, without a doubt, still to come, God consciously chose to whisper these words to Jeremiah:

"Call to me and I will answer you and tell you great and unsearchable things you do not know."

If Jeremiah had asked and then listened, he might've heard and seen the *"great and unsearchable things"* that God already had in mind:

- The faithful, future rebuilding of the Temple by the Israelites.

- Daniel's ministry to the Babylonian and Medo-Persian kings.

- Ezra's spiritual leadership in renewing belief in the Israelites' individual hearts.

- Nehemiah's work in turning exiles and abandoned Israelites into stouthearted up-builders of a new Israel.

Now imagine yourself fast-forwarding human history to a particular Thursday night, in the very same capital city of Jerusalem:

- The Roman authorities and armies dominate every aspect of Jewish life.

- The Messiah, Jesus, is confined with the Sanhedrin, on the way to a morning meeting with Pilate, an appointed man of Caesar.

- Within hours:

> - Jesus will be murdered outside the walls of the city.
>
> - The Temple curtain will be torn in two.
>
> - His body, His "temple," will be wrapped and laid in a tomb.
>
> - Only the people of no account ever believed much of His teaching.
>
> - The rest of humanity never saw Him, never heard from Him, never knew Him.

Yet with all of that real, and true, and, without a doubt, still to come, the Father might've whispered these words to Jesus:

"Call to me and I will answer you and tell you great and unsearchable things you and I already, together, know."

Because Jesus, being One with the Father, knowing the ways of the Holy Spirit, would've already known these coming outcomes perfectly well:

> - The temple of His body would be raised in three days.

- He would ascend to minister aside His Father in forty-three days.

- His Holy Spirit would descend, ten days after that, to uphold unconquerable belief in His believers.

- From Heaven and within, Jesus Himself would turn exiles and abandoned individuals into the stouthearted proclaimers of the Kingdom of Heaven.

Now imagine, once more, fast-forwarding all human history to the particular day in which you're sitting somewhere and reading these words:

- All sorts of personal challenges, trials, and tribulations seem to lay siege to the peace of your heart.

- You feel bound up in your circumstances, ruled over by one or another person or struggle or past choice or your life's current trajectory.

- You fear that in the future:

- It all will come to naught or to a grinding halt.

- Your dreams and accomplishments will be destroyed or mean nothing.

- Your spiritual life, thus far, won't be robust enough for your circumstances.

- You will show yourself to be a sham, a pretender; one who talked the talk, but couldn't actually walk the walk.

- God will be displeased with you.

Yet with all of that feeling real and frightening, and in your imagination still potentially to come, Jesus is whispering to you:

"Call to me and I will answer you and tell you great and unsearchable things you do not know."

Jesus—having set you free and knowing perfectly how to help you live your life—would have you experience the true reality He wants for you. That you would:

- Glory in His Cross and Resurrection (Galatians 6:14).

- Approach the throne of Heaven with His personally instilled confidence (Hebrews 4:16).

- Find the Holy Spirit within to be far mightier than any person or situation without (1 John 4:4).

- Know that He would win your orphan heart and show you the wonders of His Way; that you would become another master builder of His Kingdom (Hebrews 12:28-29).

Now imagine a day when everything I've just described is perfectly attainable, in the name of Jesus, for all those marked by the blood of Jesus.

Actually, you don't need to imagine it.
That day is—today.

Promise
18

"Have faith in God," replied Jesus to them. 'I tell you that if anyone should say to this hill, "Get up and throw yourself into the sea," and without any doubt in his heart believe that what he says will happen, then it will happen! That is why I tell you, whatever you pray about and ask for, believe that you have received it and it will be yours."'

MARK 11:22-24 PHILLIPS

With such a monumentally momentous sort of promise—ripe with wonder, rich with power—I think we need to take these words of promise in stages. So here we go:

"Have faith in God," replied Jesus to them. "*Them*" being the disciples of Jesus. "*Jesus*" being the God of Heaven, totally powerful, totally divine, and yet totally focused into the frame of a human Man. The God-Man is making a simple, verbal reply to a surprised statement they'd just uttered about a fig tree He'd just, miraculously, in the last twenty-four hours, withered to the roots. His reply, *"Have faith in God."* Have faith in *Me.* Believe what I've said before; believe what I'm saying now. Trust that, should you encounter situations where you need My heavenly power, I am presently reigning in Heaven for

you. Look toward My will in every circumstance. And, needing Me, trust Me—willfully have faith.

"I tell you that if anyone should say to this hill..."—or this situation, or circumstance, or fear, or anxiety, or need, etc....

'Get up and throw yourself into the sea'—or be altered, or be changed, or depart, or dissolve, or be resolved, etc....

"And without any doubt in his heart believe that what he says will happen..." Without any doubt. Without—any doubt. To first believe, then to encounter situations, then to look to the Lord for His will, and then to lift up prayers of trust. And then, with faith, to ask specific things that are specifically ascertainable, and then to finish your prayer with a simple "Amen." And then—right then—to not doubt, not question, not entertain those immediate thoughts of "But what if...." Instead, to believe that what He says will happen. To believe that what Jesus says, we say will happen.

*"...then it **will** happen!"* It will. Jesus just promised you that. That, having faith, aligning our life with the dynamic power of the will of God in Heaven, we may see a hill, situation, circumstance, fear, anxiety, or need and then command its removal, altering, change, departure, dissolution, or resolution. And if we simply, silently hold onto our inner resolve to trust Him, to believe, to place our faith in the Faithful One, we will see our prayer answered. Really and truly. Again, that is the promise of this promise!

"That is why I tell you..." "You," the follower of Jesus. *"I"*—Jesus—am telling you.

"*...whatever you pray about and ask for...*" Whatever. Anything. Everything. All those things that occur within the daily practice of following Jesus and that point toward the arrival of the Kingdom of Heaven. All those things that actually align with His Way. All those things that are of the straight and narrow.

"*...believe that you have received it...*" Believe. Know it. Trust Him. Lean upon the power of this promise. Lean not on your own understanding. Place the full weight of your confidence in the Man who is presently speaking these words aloud to His disciples.

"*...and it will be yours.*" Yours. By Heaven's design, it will belong to you. You have come toward the Prince of Peace with faith, trust, and belief—and He recognizes a son or daughter of God in you. There is a family resemblance you both share. And so, knowing Him, knowing of His will, knowing His heart, knowing the sorts of things that tend toward His Way, you have made a request of Him. You've simply stated what you simply need. No lengthy, talismanic-style prayers are required with Him.

You have looked Him in the eye and simply asked that you'd receive a certain change or provision or request. It has been stated to Him. It's clear between you. And then you've settled back, knowing that what He's promised He's always faithful to follow through on, and you've trusted Him. You have believed that you've already, actually received it. The prayer has been heard—and answered.

And in His perfect timing and timeliness, in an earthly experience of Heaven's all-powerful way and will, *you will receive that answer.*

It will be yours, Jesus says to you.

Have faith—*it will be yours.*

So, perhaps the only way to end this meditation is to invite you into the practice it so naturally, readily recommends:

- What is He inviting you to pray for today?

- Do you believe you can trust Him for that?

- Can you spend the next few moments laying that particular request at His feet, and then, most importantly, walking away without doubt?

Can you do that?

Then, I say...*have at it!*

Promise
19

"You can ask for anything in my name, and I will do it, so that the Son can bring glory to the Father. Yes, ask me for anything in my name, and I will do it!"

JOHN 14:13-14 NLT

Approximately forty-three days after Jesus spoke these words, He ascended back to the throne room of Heaven on a bright Jerusalem afternoon. He'd been standing on the Mount of Olives, talking to His friends, explaining the coming of the Holy Spirit, when suddenly—*He was rising toward the heavens!*

Up, up, upward He ascended as His friends all stood below; we can imagine how they strained to keep their eyes wide open, trying to take it all in. Then, reaching the clouds, disappearing from their ability to see Him anymore, Jesus was suddenly whisked away to the "right side up" that is the heavenly realm.

Personally, I've always imagined the entrance to the throne room being an enormous, brightly colored, paneled pair of doors, massive on their gilt fittings. Jesus walks right through, shoving them open. Across the infinite-and-yet-intimate distance of the hall, He then locks eyes with His Father, upon His throne, and begins His walk toward Him. The angels and saints, first hushed, erupt. They sing a song of His glory as He strides down the center aisle—trumpets blaring, harps ascendant—until He reaches the very dais.

Then all is silent.

All wait.

Jesus raises His human foot.

Takes the first step.

Then the second.

And the third.

And then, with a smile that shines with all the heavenly glory and earthly relief of having completed His salvation work, Jesus retakes His seat on the throne. He walks those last few steps and turns around, gathers His train, looks out into the sea of faces—and sits down. Down upon the seat on which He'd always sat. Down into the comfort of where He'd created Creation. Back inside the hall where all divine dominion resides. Back beside His Father—that other part of Himself.

But then in a move that must've made all His heavenly watchers watch Him in wonder, He did something rather curious: He leaned far forward almost to the very front edge of His throne. His head started tilting to one side like He was listening for something in particular, and all Heaven waited to see what it might be…

* * *

After suddenly seeing their Friend ascend and depart behind the clouds, the disciples stayed right where they were. With hands cupped around their eyes, blocking out all extraneous light, they just kept hoping that they might catch one more glimpse of Him—which explains their total nonchalance when two angelic beings arrive. A casual conversation ensues, man-to-angel, and the disciples were told to head back into Jerusalem to wait for the power promised by Jesus.

I've always imagined them walking back down a narrow trail on the western slope of the Mount of Olives, down through its twists and turns into the Kidron Valley, down through where, perhaps, on the night before the Cross, Jesus had turned toward a run of vines and said, "I am the vine, you are the branches." Then, up the disciples climb, up, up, upward toward the eastern wall of the city, toward a spot with a partial view of Herod's Temple. Then, entering by a gate, meandering almost mindlessly through the maze of narrow streets, they arrive to where the morning had started out. Back to the "upper room," as they've come to call that space.

They climb the stairs, enter through the narrow door, and take their places around the room—some in chairs, some upon reed mats on the floor. The others who were not part of the hike and picnic on the Mount of Olives are looking around, wondering where Jesus is. But no one says a word—yet. No one moves. The room is totally still.

Then the Eleven, almost as one, rise to their feet, cross the room and assemble in circle at the center of this, the whole earthly fellowship of Jesus of Nazareth. They study each other's faces for the same thought and understanding. They all wonder if the others are thinking what they're thinking.

Then one of them—was it Peter? Was it John? Was it an unexpected one like Simon the Zealot?—begins to pray aloud…

He closes his eyes.

He lifts both hands.

But he prays a prayer that has never been prayed in the whole of human history: a prayer that is perfectly in accordance with their perfect understanding of today's promise.

"Jesus," he prays, "it's us. All of us."

*   *   *

And as He hears those words, Jesus Himself leans back upon the throne of Heaven, smiling to Himself, and knows that all will be well.

The Holy Spirit is only ten days away.

The Kingdom of Heaven is now embedded firmly within those hearts.

And now, understanding the power of His name, knowing that they can always call—*anytime*—His friends have opened the direct channel of communication.

Earth to Heaven, that open Way is Jesus.

His name holds all the power of Heaven.

"You can ask for anything in my name, and I will do it, so that the Son can bring glory to the Father. Yes, ask me for anything in my name, and I will do it!"

Shall we, seriously, take Him up on this promise today?

Promise
20

"You did not choose me, but I chose you and appointed you that you should go and bear fruit and that your fruit should abide, so that whatever you ask the Father in my name, he may give it to you"

John 15:16 ESV

One of the greatest enemies of practicable discipleship—fulsome following of Jesus of Nazareth—is that deadly, almost unnoticed feeling of creeping overfamiliarity. You'll know the feeling is present when you're either listening to, or when you're personally reading through words like these in John 15, and find yourself *not* stunned by them. That is the work of overfamiliarity.

Overfamiliarity is the product of a conscious, or unconscious, thought process whereby we think we already know all there is to know of something. So, reading of that subject again, one's mind somewhat shuts down. An unthinking instinct seems to take over—like when you sometimes arrive at home without totally remembering your drive there—and Jesus' words become a sort of background to one's thoughts.

Words like *choose, chose, appointed, go, bear fruit, abide, in My name*, get filtered out by the noise of whatever the day holds.

Let us together say: *Not today!*

Today, I would have us wrestling with, and reveling in, the glorious practicalities of fulsome following after that wonderful Man, Jesus of Nazareth. And I want to take two particular different angles on today's promise so that these words become a bit unfamiliar, fresh, and new.

To do that, instead of Jesus speaking these words *to you* in the second person plural (you, as in "all of you many"), we will speak these words aloud *to Him* in two different voices: the first person singular ("I" and "me") and the first person plural ("us" and "we"). We'll do this because, in the day-to-day context in which we live our lives and follow His Way, we often tend to be His disciples very much on our own. And this is natural: He *means* to lead us individually—and powerfully.

And yet, if we want to overwhelm the world with the wonder of His glory, and really show His Church in the power of its full manifestation, we absolutely *must* reconstitute the Body of Christ—and properly.

So here's the plan:

I want you to read aloud, with some authority, the two new versions of these verses (1st person, singular and plural) and what I want you to do is—get carried away!

Repeat these words aloud—loudly—with your whole heart and mind; strip that latent overfamiliarity right out of the equation—make them today's battle cry! Believe what you're hearing and pronouncing. Pronounce what you desire to believe as you hear it.

Here you go—take it away:

Jesus, I did not choose You, but You chose me and appointed me that I should go and bear fruit and that my fruit should abide, so that whatever I ask the Father in Your name, He may give it to me.

And, as a member of the Body of Christ, say this:

Jesus, we did not choose You, but You chose us and appointed us that we should go and bear fruit and that our fruit should abide, so that whatever we ask the Father in Your name, He may give it to us.

My friend, as a member of the Body, and as an integral part of the constantly re-coalescing Whole that is Him, you did not choose—you are chosen. In fact, being chosen, not being in a position powerful enough to choose, Jesus instead decided to appoint you to the most powerful position He could find for you—a messenger of the Gospel and a bearer of its fruit. And that fruit, by the way, will abide—*as you abide in Him.* And, too, just in case the foregoing information wasn't enough to stun your sensibilities, you may ask whatever you wish of the Father in Heaven—the heavenly Father—*and He will give it to you.*

Now what do you think of all *that?*

Isn't this promise too absolutely awe-inspiring?

Promise
21

"In that day you will no longer ask Me anything. Truly, truly, I tell you, whatever you ask the Father in My name, He will give you. Until now you have not asked for anything in My name. Ask and you will receive, so that your joy may be complete."

JOHN 16:23-24 BSB

Imagine yourself in a cemetery—a burial ground. It is early morning: the air is cool with the remnants of the night; a mist still hugs the ground and encircles the canopies of the low trees. As you walk, you can actually watch the way the fog is moved by your movements, how it parts and swirls with the swish of your garments. You begin walking slower. You are very nearly there: to the tomb of the Man you were certain was the One: all the feelings begin rising again in your heart. All your hopes and future visions—dashed—all the anguish of the day before yesterday, are right back in front of you. The image of His bloodied near-nakedness; the sounds of the scoffers; that final picture in your mind of the moment He simply went limp. How He sagged against the nails and His body leaned forward. That man and that Pharisee coming to wrap Him up...to bring Him to this place, right in front of you.

Just another bend in the path and you'll see it again.

On Friday evening, you had followed those two men, carting the Body over this very path, and had watched the way they, and their crowds of servants, had sealed the mouth of the tomb.

Now that tomb and its sealing stone are almost in view.

Except—

It's open.

The mouth of the tomb of Jesus is agape: wide and black.

Without even thinking, you begin to run right back the way you just slowly walked. You must tell the others of this horrific, criminal act of grave-robbing! Peter and John and the others must be told!

And yet, half an hour later, having told Peter and John—who then went running out to the spot—you are right back at the spot yourself. Those two had gone running off and disappeared, and yet, on your way back here, just now, they went right by you without saying a word to you. Peter was shaking his head and whispering aloud to himself. John's eyes were aglow—yet he walked right by.

And so, now, steeling your spirit, battening down your fears, you are walking toward the mouth of the tomb to see what there is to see of His last resting place. You stoop your head and squint your eyes to acclimate to the complete darkness of the tomb and you—

Oh!

You reel back in fear! There are suddenly two bright men, shining in clothing and countenance, sitting inside the empty tomb, one at the head, one at the foot, of the bloody slab where the Body had been!

"Why are you crying?" one of them asks you.

"They have stolen away my Lord," you reply. "And I don't know where His body is."

And right then from behind you, you suddenly experience that prickly neck feeling of feeling the presence of another person unexpectedly near you where they just weren't. You wheel quickly almost hitting your head on the top of the mouth of the tomb—and there He is, this unexpected Person. He is standing where the rising sun is wrapping His body in light; where the only view of His face and body is a black darkness.

"Why are you crying?" this Man also asks.

Your answer is nearly the same—but also includes accusation. For if this Man is the gardener (as you're starting to guess He might be) then He may be part of the plot to remove Jesus' body from the tomb. You feel a sort of indignation within you as you answer Him: "Sir, if you've carried Him away, tell me to where. I will come, myself, and take Him away."

A silence follows your statement...

Then, stepping toward you, stepping into the shadowing space at the fringe of an olive tree, the Man comes a step nearer.

"*Mary!*" the voice of Jesus says.

You run to Him so as not to collapse to the ground...

"In that day you will no longer ask Me anything. Truly, truly, I tell you, whatever you ask the Father in My name, He will give you. Until now you have not asked for anything in My name. Ask and you will receive, so that your joy may be complete."

It's been my observation that when we read these words from the night of the Last Discourse, sitting in comfortable quiet-time spots or Sunday morning pews, we tend to focus on the middle clauses of those verses—*asking whatever we want, receiving answers in His name*, etc.—rather than on the reality in which *all prayers* are now prayed.

Where are *all prayers* prayed now?

On the other side of "that day"—that glorious, misty morning when Mary encountered Him again—when all earthly and heavenly joy was made forever *"complete."* On this side of human history where sin, satan, death, and the grave hold absolutely no power; where righteousness, Jesus, life, and eternity are the final words.

And I love how Jesus painted the picture of Mary's posture three nights before that morning, when He said, *"In that day you will no longer ask Me anything."* After all, when you're clasping the feet of the Man who's defeated death, you are not too apt to lift up paltry sorts of prayer requests anymore. Your heavenly joy overwhelms all perception of earthly need. If He can do *this*, He can do any kind of *that*.

The men and women who followed closely after Him in that century—The Early Church—were never *not* alight with the complete joy that morning kindled. In fact, their lives were its ever-ready afterglow. Their prayers were offered up in full remembrance of the new reality.

My friend, the higher intimacy we ourselves enjoy with a present, alive Savior, the more meaningfully unimportant all else but Him will become. Clasping His feet like Mary, we become more and more lost in Him. In His Way. In His will. In His ever-present midst.

Let us be the sort of people who encounter Him first—first thing in the morning before all else, and then let's later see what still needs to be prayed for. Let's let our prayers be dictated by *"that day"* and by a joy so *"complete"* that all else pales in earthly comparison.

As Jesus then said to Mary, *"Go and tell my brothers that I am going up to my Father and your Father, to my God and your God"* (John 20:17 Phillips).

Let us go and show and tell the very same today.

Remember—this day is *this* side of *"that day."*

Promise 22

"When the poor and needy search for water and there is none, and their tongues are parched from thirst, then I, the Lord, will answer them. I, the God of Israel, will never abandon them. I will open up rivers for them on the high plateaus. I will give them fountains of water in the valleys. I will fill the desert with pools of water. Rivers fed by springs will flow across the parched ground"

ISAIAH 41:17-18 NLT

First things first, I don't believe in spiritual "seasons." I won't submit to that churchly analogy—however cleverly it's spoken. I will literally leave from a sermon wherein the pastor wants me to acquiesce in accepting "dry seasons," "down times," and "dark nights of the soul." And, please understand me: This is *not* because I've never experienced the feeling of feeling dry, in an emotional abyss, or walking through my own share of overwhelming darkness. Along with all of you, I've been there, I've done that.

No, the reason I will not accept *accepting* dry, down, dark "seasons" is because of promises like these; New Covenants like ours.

Allow me to explain more fully.

When the aforementioned *"poor and needy search for water and there is none,"* they are representative of every man, woman, and child searching for spiritual reality and yet not finding their way to God. Spiritual poverty is equivalent to unmet spiritual thirst; and the worst place to be thirsty is in a land with no water, no wells.

But being thirsty, with tongues dry and parched, this promise clearly states that the thirsty prayers of these people will be answered. The *"God of Israel will never abandon them"*—and, instead, will do what? *"Open up rivers for them on the high plateaus"* and *"give them **fountains** of water in the valleys"* and *"**fill** the desert with pools of water."* The topography of their dry, thirsty, inner lives will become like *"Rivers fed by springs"* that *"flow across the parched ground."*

That is the sparkling joy of this beautiful promise.

But let's take it even a step further.

On a certain day, sitting in a small, Samaritan town, waiting beside its central well, Jesus spoke these words to an incredulous woman, *"If you knew the gift of God and who it is that asks you for a drink, you would have asked him and he would have given you living water"* (John 4:10 NIV). To which she demurs, pointing out His lack of ladle or bucket, plus His scarcity of seeming status when compared to the patriarch Jacob who'd provided said well. Jesus is not put off by her arguments. He goes on, *"Everyone who drinks this water will be thirsty again, but **whoever drinks the water I give them will never thirst**. Indeed, the water I give them will become in them a spring of water welling up to eternal life"* (John 4:13-14 NIV).

Then not too many months later, standing in the Temple at the center of all Jewish worship, Jesus again says, *"Let anyone who is thirsty come to me and drink. Whoever believes in me, as Scripture has said, **rivers of living water will flow from within them**"* (John 7:37-38 NIV). And the apostle John, worried that we'd struggle to connect the spiritual dots between these references to spiritual water, then drops his readers a little aside: *"By this [Jesus] meant the Spirit, whom those who believed in him were later to receive. Up to that time the Spirit had not been given, since Jesus had not yet been glorified"* (John 7:39 NIV).

But Jesus has now *"been glorified,"* hasn't He?

And the Spirit has now *"been given,"* right?

This Spirit is the *"rivers of living water"* that *"flow from within,"* the One who comes to those who believe in Jesus. Those who were thirsty came to Him to drink; this Spirit is a *"spring of water welling up to eternal life,"* the water Jesus gives and by which we may *"never thirst."* This Holy Spirit of Jesus is the *"living water,"* and according to Jesus Himself we may simply ask for Him. He is the fulfillment of the promise, as spoken to Isaiah, in the words we call Isaiah 41:17-18! The Holy Spirit is the actual living key to unlocking every part of today's promise!

In fact, I might render that promise this way:

When the spiritually poor and needy search for spiritual answers and yet find none, and their tongues are parched from spiritual thirst, then I, the Lord Jesus, will answer them. I, the God of the universe, will never abandon them. I will pour out my Spirit, opening up rivers for their souls in the heavenly high plateaus. I will give them fountains of my Spirit in the valleys of their inner lives. I will fill the dry, down, dark deserts of their spirits with my Holy Spirit. Rivers fed by springs that flow from the throne of God will flow across their parched ground—forever.

My friend, the reason I will not submit to any, even the cleverest, analogy of seasons, valleys, or darknesses is because of promises like these. I will not allow my spirit to ignore the presence of the Holy Spirit who is living water, a spring, fountain, and river by which I never need thirst again. And while I am not belittling the challenges we all face—especially as I'm writing this in the midst of a global pandemic—I will not bow my knee to them.

- *No season is stronger than Jesus of Nazareth.*
- *No thirst is left unquenchable in His presence.*
- *All dark nights can be lit up by His Spirit.*

But…we must go to Him and ask, believe, receive, drink, and be filled, if we want, as promised, to never thirst again. We must let the Holy Spirit be the spring, fountain, and river of living water that He's been promised to us to be.

Shall we let Him be Himself today?

Promise
23

"It shall come to pass that before they call, I will answer; and while they are still speaking, I will hear."

ISAIAH 65:24 NKJV

Over these sheltered-in-place months, I've been reading in history, philosophy, fiction, and theology—really wonderful voices as varied as Thomas Aquinas, Montaigne, Napoleon, Thoreau, and C.S. Lewis. But the perspective, aside from Scripture, that has most drawn my heart to the Lord has been that of the Stoic philosopher, Epictetus, who lived during the same time as the Early Church. I couldn't stop myself from reading right through his *Fragments*, then all the way through all four of his *Discourses*. And I found myself consistently moved by two things: his relentlessness in trying to look to God, and his total resignation in giving himself over to the will of that God.

Epictetus lived a true self-abandonment life. He firmly believed that the will of God would practically lead and guide him. If he prayed a prayer, it was for a greater personal understanding *that God already knew* and that he (Epictetus) might *more fully reside in God's will and provision.*

What a beautiful posture to see in a "virtuous pagan."

In fact, if you'll humor me, I'd like you to read a few stretches of his best writings on those subjects—slowly read his words and then I'll offer a short thought or two. Then we'll circle back to the connection with today's promise and an activity for which you'll need the lined space provided.

So, here we go—Epictetus on God and trust:

> Lift up your neck at last like a man escaped from bondage, be bold to look towards God and say, "Use me henceforward for whatever [You will]; I am of one mind with [You]; I am [Yours]; I crave exemption from nothing that seems good in [Your] sight; where [You will], lead me; in what raiment [You will], clothe me. [Would you] have me to hold office, or remain in private life; to remain here or go into exile; to be poor, to be rich? I will defend all these [Your] acts before men; I will show what the truest nature of each thing is."[1]

Or, in other words: You have already set me free from bondage; Your sovereign will is always truly good and right. So, now, I bind myself to You: I want nothing that You don't, Yourself, give. And I will always point everyone to the true goodness of Your ways.

Next:

> I have considered all this, no one has authority over me. I have been set free by God, I know His commands, no one has power any longer to make

a slave of me, I have the right kind of emancipator, and the right kind of judge…

…I regard God's will as better than my will. I shall attach myself to Him as a servant and follower, my choice is one with His, my desire one with His, in a word, my will is one with His will.[2]

Or, in other words: Being free, *I will be free.* The One who emancipated me is the very One who also will judge. And so I attach the full weight of my will to the fuller understanding of His will. His will is everything. *His* will is life itself.

Then:

Does God so neglect His own creatures, His servants, His witnesses, whom alone He uses as examples to the uninstructed, to prove that He both is, and governs the universe well, and does not neglect the affairs of men, and that no evil befalls a good man either in life or in death? …I obey, I follow, lauding my commander, and singing hymns of praise about His deeds. For I came into the world when it so pleased Him, and I leave it again at His pleasure, and while I live this was my function—to sing hymns of praise unto God, to myself and to others, be it to one or to many.[3]

Or, in other words: Our individual lives are the proof-point for all the wonders and glories of our God. Let our song, then, as evidences of Him, be ever after only praises unto Him.

And, finally:

...For [the reason you created] me I am grateful; for what [You have] given I am grateful also. The lengths of time for which I have had the use of [Your] gifts is enough for me. Take them back again and assign them to what place [You will], for they were all [Yours], and [You gave] them me." Is it not enough for a man to take his departure from the world in this state of mind? And what among all the kinds of life is superior to this, or more seemly than he who is so minded, and what kind of end is more fortunate?[4]

Or, in other words: In life and in death, what could be better than gratitude, trust, and absolute surrender to the will of God? Is anything finer than to know His power and character, and to, there, place the full weight of your hope upon Him?

So in that same spirit of surrender and trust, what are we to do with the God who—before we even have the chance to call or speak—is already in the process of answering? How should we be learning to trust the Savior who is presently leaning forward at the edge of His throne, not wanting to miss even a whisper of the beginning of one of our simplest prayers?

How?

In what way?

I say, *by engaging.*

And I would add, *by doing.*

On the pages that follow, on the left-hand side of the page, I want you to write down *every present prayer request* you can think of—no matter how great or small. Try not to leave anything out that's been on your mind.

And then, opposite each prayer request, I want you to make note of *what it actually means to you* that, not only is He leaning forward to hear that prayer, not only does He already know the entirety of that request, not only does He already know all the circumstances involved in the lead up to and the making of that request, He has already—in His perfect knowledge—*made an answer.* What does that mean to you? How does it change your posture within that prayer?

Endnotes

1. Epictetus, trans. W.A. Oldfather, *The Discourses, Books I and II* (Cambridge, MA: Harvard University Press, 1925).

2. Epictetus, trans. W.A. Oldfather, *The Discourses, Books III-IV, Fragments & Encheiridion* (Cambridge, MA: Harvard University Press, 1928).

3. Ibid.

4. Ibid.

Answered Prayer

Promise
24

"In a certain town there was a judge who neither feared God nor cared what people thought. And there was a widow in that town who kept coming to him with the plea, 'Grant me justice against my adversary.' For some time he refused. But finally he said to himself, 'Even though I don't fear God or care what people think, yet because this widow keeps bothering me, I will see that she gets justice, so that she won't eventually come and attack me!' And the Lord said, 'Listen to what the unjust judge says. And will not God bring about justice for his chosen ones, who cry out to him day and night? Will he keep putting them off? I tell you, he will see that they get justice, and quickly. However, when the Son of Man comes, will he find faith on the earth?'"

LUKE 18:2-8 NIV

Or, I'll put it to you another way:

In a certain Heaven there was a Judge who was God and who cared overwhelmingly, absolutely for His people. At a particular point in time, that very God—the so-called Judge—had, in fact, made His way to come and visit and walk among His people. He was sent into the world not *"to condemn the world, but to save the world through"* the gift of His very own life (John 3:17 NIV). His *"Father judges no one, but [had] entrusted all judgment to [Him], that all may honor the Son just as they honor the Father"* (John 5:22-23 NIV). And very truly He told us that, *"whoever hears my word and believes him who sent me has eternal life and will not be judged but has crossed over from death to life"* (John 5:24 NIV).

So, so much for thinking of Him as only a Judge!

But let's get back to where we were, in my version of today's promise...

And there was a person upon the earth who kept coming to Him with the prayer, "Please take care of me in this or that regard." For *no time* did He refuse this request. He kept blessing and providing and bringing peace to this or that situation the person kept bringing to Him. And then He revealed Himself more fully to that person, "Even though I'm not sure you totally understand Me, and I certainly see how much you care what people think, yet because I am entirely good—goodness being my innate essence, after all—I will continue to answer your prayers, provide for you, care for you in every day of your earthly life, but, even more importantly, as you trust Me more, I will reveal myself to you more. Come, come, keep coming, I say! The more you're in My presence, the more of Me you'll get!" And this Lord also said, "Listen to what the just Judge says. For does not my Father bring about justice and peace and righteousness and joy and hope for His chosen ones, who cry out to Him day and night? Will He keep listening to them and drawing them closer? Of course He will! I tell you, He is always seeing that they get justice and peace and righteousness and joy and hope, and quickly. Yet I must ask the question: when the Son of Man comes again, will He find faith on the earth?"

When you consider this promise, this parable, from the angle of the *already accomplished, eternal work of Jesus,* doesn't it make your heart beat just a little bit faster? On the day of His original speaking, Jesus used the "unjust judge" as a counterpoint to the justice of God; today, I have taken us a little further into the overall equation. For not only is He just and good and inviting us ever closer, inviting our prayers of any and all kinds of metrics or measure—*He wants us.* He wants our prayer to be not the plaintive cries of the persistent widow, unsure of the unjust judge's response—He wants our unflappable confidence. He desires to hear from men, women, and children who enjoy His presence, who want more of Him, who, by proximity, desire intimacy born of experience, acceptance, and duration-in-nearness.

That's what He wants in your prayer life.

What do *you* want in your prayer life?

Do you *only* desire to see your needs, concerns, and provision taken care of, right now, directly?

Or, along with that, do you *also* desire to talk to One you intimately trust, intimately know, and to grow more into His likeness?

Do you *only* want to know that you're always heard, always provided for, always taken care of—and yet do you *actually*, then, just want to "get back to your life"?

Or, having been heard, having been provided for, always taken care of—do you also want to experience His life overtaking, and taking over your life?

Are you familiar with the ways and means involved, *"when the Son of Man comes,"* that "[He will] find faith on the earth"? Do you know the means and manner of creating a faithful atmosphere on earth; of working to found, establish, and build His Kingdom *"on earth as it is in Heaven"?* Do you know the building blocks that build the Church to be faithful, prayerful, trusting, and true, for the eventual return of Jesus, the King of the Kingdom?

You.

You are the building block.

You are the means and the manner.

You are the place where—Jesus looking—faith may be found on the earth during this particular day we call today.

So what are *you* looking for in prayer when you talk to Him?

For answers—or intimacy?

For transactions—or glory?

Let this promise draw your heart a little higher today.

Section Five

PRACTICAL PROVISION

Promise
25

"Ask, and it will be given to you; seek, and you will find; knock, and it will be opened to you. For everyone who asks receives, and he who seeks finds, and to him who knocks it will be opened. Or what man is there among you who, if his son asks for bread, will give him a stone? Or if he asks for a fish, will he give him a serpent? If you then, being evil, know how to give good gifts to your children, how much more will your Father who is in heaven give good things to those who ask Him!"

MATTHEW 7:7-11 NKJV

It is early morning in a small house in the Galilee. You are standing in the area where food is prepared. A long wooden counter runs along the length of the wall and ends with a small cooking stove, standing in the corner. Centered above the middle of the counter is a square-cut window, carved out of the wall, looking out over the Sea. The morning air is ruffling the surface of the waters, traveling over the reeds and rushes, and then through the window, cooling the room. A woman, your mother, stands directly before the window, preparing a meal for you, her son, who stands back of her. She has very nearly finished making your lunch.

"What is it?" you ask.

"The usual," she says. "With a little extra, besides." She turns. "And when you meet your cousins, stay on the main road, stay with the crowds, and don't get lost on the way—promise?"

You nod your head, yes.

She kisses you goodbye. "Stay with the crowds," she says again.

And then you're out the door and up the narrow street and onto the main road, traveling north, with the foothills on your left; the Sea on your right. You are almost running, you're so excited. The sea breeze continues to blow and toss the grass and wildflowers in wild concentric circles; the dust of the road, now and then, gusts up in a cloud.

Up ahead, you can finally see the crowds. Enormous, *enormous* crowds of people!

At the back of the crowd you can see your four cousins, waiting behind, probably hanging back until, as they'd promised, they find you. Meeting up, you all move forward together. The crowd continues its great migration until it reaches the meadow near Bethsaida. In that meadow, at its upper northwestern edge, sitting on a rise of ground atop a rock, is Jesus from Nazareth, the Teacher everyone's traveled to see. You and the whole countryside have wanted to see Him and to hear Him. You first heard of Jesus when His disciples came through your town and healed a friend's grandmother in His name. And there is He is, now. In the flesh. Beginning to teach from His meadow perch.

From where you are, you can only hear a little of the words He's speaking—and hearing a little of Jesus is *not* why you came up here today. So, leaving your cousins, who didn't notice, and skirting the edge of the vast crowds, you make your way nearer and nearer toward the Teacher. You continue creeping your way around the southern side of the people—winding your way through a small grove of trees—and, popping out, *there He is!* You have actually moved to within ten or fifteen feet of where He's sitting. You settle down, with your back against a juniper, and begin listening again…

The day passes…

The words are everything you heard they'd be…

Marvelous stories of birds and flowers and people and hills…

The Kingdom of Heaven…

The idea of actually knowing God…

The chance, you realize, to personally get to follow after Him…

Oh, Jesus is so good!

You're so swept up in all your listening to Him, thinking about His Father, following the stories as closely as you can, that you realize you never ate your lunch. Now dusk is starting to drop. And Jesus has suddenly stopped teaching.

"Where will we find the bread to feed these people?" you hear Him ask.

One of His disciples responds, "Two hundred denarii wouldn't do it, Jesus!"

Then, there is quiet conversation in their midst. You are watching from the shade of your juniper tree...

Until—rising up, gathering up your courage, taking a deep breath and letting it out, you begin walking toward them.

You didn't come today, you didn't leave your cousins and the crowd behind to not do something that would make this day a "day of days." *This will be the day you talk to Jesus!* This will be the day you offer Him what you have. Regardless of the thousands of people stretching as far as the eye can see, you have food that you'd like to offer to Jesus. Five loaves and two fish. It's not a lot—but this is Jesus, after all...

*   *   *

My friend, given today's promise, why do I bring John 6 to mind? Why, when we're reading of *asking, seeking, knocking, being given good things by Him,* am I drawing your imagination to giving something *to* Him? Why, in our shift toward considering promises of provision, am I asking you to consider an act of yielding, of relinquishing, instead?

Because that little boy's act is the great promise of this promise. Because, as described, his day that day is the pattern we're after.

You and I will truly find the glory of these words when, leaving behind all crowds, friends, and family, *we personally find Jesus.* When we've heard His words for ourselves, when we've gained a sense of His nearness, we're beginning to get closer to the joyousness of this promise. When He turns His gaze upon us, beckoning us nearer and nearer and nearer, we can almost see the fulfillment of these words. We're very nearly there now...

You see, it's only when we realize we can release our need-for-provision to Jesus that we get to watch the way He feeds the world—*and us*. Our intimacy becomes our access to watching how our trust in Him begets trust in others; provision, peace, hope in others. Leaving the crowds behind, we actually help to feed the crowds. Trusting Jesus for ourselves, *we show everyone a new heavenly path of provision.*

This day is your opportunity to practice acting in the manner of that little boy: Will you get close to Jesus? Will you move outside the crowd, past all friends and family? Will you let nothing stand in the way of your nearness to Him? Will you get to where, no matter what the day holds, you can still hear the sound of His voice for yourself?

And, most importantly—will you trust Him there? Will you literally trust that it's His job to feed you? Will you give Him opportunity to provide, using you, using your trust, using your means, so that the whole world can see? Will you believe in His provisionary abilities in such a way that all the world—your friends and family—can see heavenly provision in practice?

Hear Him once again: *"**how much more** will your Father who is in heaven give good things to those who ask Him!"*

Have you yourself already asked Him?

Then, today is the very time to trust, believe, wait, receive—and tomorrow it'll be time for showing and telling.

Today, bring Him only your trust.

And let Him show the world what He can do with it.

Promise
26

"*Therefore I tell you, do not be anxious about your life, what you will eat or what you will drink, nor about your body, what you will put on. Is not life more than food, and the body more than clothing? Look at the birds of the air: they neither sow nor reap nor gather into barns, and yet your heavenly Father feeds them. Are you not of more value than they? And which of you by being anxious can add a single hour to his span of life? And why are you anxious about clothing? Consider the lilies of the field, how they grow: they neither toil nor spin, yet I tell you, even Solomon in all his glory was not arrayed like one of these. But if God so clothes the grass of the field, which today is alive and tomorrow is thrown into the oven, will he not much more clothe you, O you of little faith? Therefore do not be anxious, saying, 'What shall we eat?' or 'What shall we drink?' or 'What shall we wear?' For the Gentiles seek after all these things, and your heavenly Father knows that you need them all. But seek first the kingdom of God and his righteousness, and all these things will be added to you. Therefore do not be anxious about tomorrow, for tomorrow will be anxious for itself. Sufficient for the day is its own trouble."*

MATTHEW 6:25-34 ESV

I've always wanted to expand upon these wonderful verses "from the inside"—to bring them further to life while walking around in the midst of their glories. Well, here's my chance:

> *"Therefore..."* A word which, whenever spoken, always casts us backward. What came before it that lends weight to what's now coming? Take a look: *"No one can serve two masters, for either he will hate the one and love the other, or he will be devoted to the one and despise the other. You cannot serve God and money"* (Matthew 6:24 ESV). So, assuming we're not twenty-six days into this study for the purpose of following money, let's be seriously ready to pay attention to what Jesus says next: *"I tell you..."* Jesus tells you; Jesus tells us. This is the Incarnate God of the universe, looking you directly in the eye, wanting to make sure that you understand what He's about to say, *"do not be anxious about your life..."* A stated, verbal command for all time.

And, as a follower of Jesus, wanting to draw nearer to Him, wanting to show the world His goodness, this is also the perfect place to begin. After all, imagine practically anyone you know who doesn't know Him. Actually, imagine practically anyone at all. The state of the world is a constant repetition of bad news, troubles, reasons to worry, and, for that reason, they're constantly worried. They're worried about today, next week, ten years from now; their job, its benefits, their eventual retirement; their family, their friends, nearly every relationship in their life. So, how might it impact their understanding of the practical goodness of a Carpenter-Teacher who lived 2,000 years ago if, when they happen to see you, you happen to be without worry? If the very same constant barrage of bad news, troubles, reasons to worry, give you not the slightest palpitation or any apparent trouble at all?

And yet, how will we get there? Jesus gets specific: *"what you will eat or what you will drink"*—by not worrying about putting food on the table; *"nor about your body, what you will put on"* meaning, your clothing, household items, etc. And then He's got a pragmatic sort of question for you: *"Is not life more than food, and the body more than clothing?"* To which you'd have to admit: Yes. It appears that life is literally more than food and clothing, Jesus. Especially when we look at the over-the-top qualities of the deep daily living You Yourself once did upon earth. Which makes me wonder if He Himself had any personal practices that helped Him?

I wonder, again speaking pragmatically, if He Himself took certain consistent steps within His human journey that helped Him not to worry? Well, I think He did: *"Look at the birds of the air: they neither sow nor reap nor gather into barns, and yet your heavenly Father feeds them."* This is one of my personally favorite commands, and potential personal practices, of Jesus—looking at the birds of the air.

In a worried week or on an anxious day, walk outside your office or your house and simply tilt your head upward to watch the absolutely unconcerned movements of a bird's day: the way they flit and fly with a perpetual song on their beak. How they feather their nests and gather up their next meal with nothing in the whole world to make them anxious at all. *Our Heavenly Father feeds them!* And, *"Are you not of more value than they?"* A rhetorical question straight from Jesus!

Clearly, He has no interest in us digging down deep in our troubled, neurotic, self-concerned selves to come back with an actual answer to this simple question. The question is rhetorical; it needs no answer. Of course we are of more value than a bunch of birds! Which is the exact place Jesus wants your heart before this saying, *"And which of you by being anxious can add a single hour to his span of life?"* Less rhetorical, now, than purposely provoking. Now He's placing His hand upon our shoulder with a slightly laughing smile upon his lips, and attacking the basis of our consistent worry.

We literally believe that worrying for our life is somehow productive; that the time we've spent worrying in a day somehow moves our day—or our future—forward. According to Jesus, it doesn't. It didn't. It never has. Every single minute we worry, according to Jesus of Nazareth, is a minute we've wasted.

Then He gets specific again: *"And why are you anxious about clothing?"* And He's not referring here to how you look or how feel about your appearance. He's talking about your worry for the provision of clothing, staple goods, everyday needs that cloud your every day.

In that space: *"Consider the lilies of the field, how they grow..."* Probably my second, personally favorite command, and potential personal practice of Jesus—considering the flowers. In a worried week, or on an anxious day, walk outside your office or your house and simply tilt your head downward to watch the absolutely unbothered, gorgeous-looking way in which the Lord has set the flowers apart in their careless beauty. How they waft with the breezes unconcernedly. How they brighten all life by the simple act of existing.

"They neither toil nor spin, yet I tell you, even Solomon in all his glory was not arrayed like one of these." Which is no offense to King Solomon; he certainly tried. Yet the mindless flowers still beat him. *"But if God so clothes the grass of the field, which today is alive and tomorrow is thrown into the oven, will he not much more clothe you, O you of little faith?"* Which has us back again to a head-nodding rhetorical question. Back to Jesus baiting our self-centric worry. Back to how He views it every time we think to ourselves, *But this time, He really might not...*

As it pertains to how we clothe ourselves, feed ourselves, go about the business of being human, Jesus wants us simply to accept His provision as a matter of course. He wants us taking stout, inward measures for ensuring that all our thoughts of all of that, become only thoughts of Him, our Provider.

After all, continue reading: *"Therefore do not be anxious"*—another statement of that same first command. But this time with qualifiers: *"saying, 'What shall we eat?' or 'What shall we drink?' or 'What shall we wear?'"* And I'd even add a few more: "Do I have enough saved?" or "Will I get that promotion?" or 'Will my daughter make that competitive, traveling team?' or "What does that person *really* think of me?" or "What did he mean by that last thing he said?" or "Will I be impoverished in my clearly deserved, long-hard-fought-for retirement in my latter (realistically-speaking, unpromised) years of life?"

In that vein, He goes on, *"For the Gentiles [the unbelievers] seek after all these things"* which is another strong provoking statement from Jesus. In essence: Why are you worried about the exact same things that all the people who don't know Me are consistently worried about? You and I are off to other, better, eternal, Kingdom things now—don't you understand that?

And then comes the clincher statement of all clincher statements: *"and your heavenly Father knows that you need them all."* He knows. He literally knows. There is not a question of work, bills, mortgages, clothing, future, traveling teams, retirement, dreams, difficult bosses, startup ventures, marriage, children, food on the table, or roofs over heads that He doesn't already intimately know.

The question is: *Do you actually believe that?* Do you believe that your own heavenly Father actually knows what you need and that He's practically concerned with taking care of you to a T? Do you believe that He is precise in His provision? That He knows exactly what you need, when you need it, for your best good? That He's doing something absolutely cosmic with your daily activities? That the way that He's providing for your life is actually part of how He's showing the world the nature of His goodness? And so, presuming you'll say yes to all that, where do you and I now fit in?

"But seek first the kingdom of God and his righteousness" which are only possible when walking the Way of Jesus with Jesus; *"and all these things will be added to you."* Sweet words, those! Or, to put them another way: If you simply, daily follow the Way of Jesus, establishing as you do the Kingdom of God and His righteousness, then all the needs of life will fall into your lap. No need to qualify, or clarify, that statement. No need to worry about your "traditional American values" either. Followers of Jesus are no longer cogs in the mechanics of the capitalist system; they are not beholden to anyone for their daily bread. Anyone, of course, other than their heavenly Father: the Maker of the earth and the heavens, of all life, of all human life. That One is your only actual boss now. And your only heavenly Provider.

"Therefore…" all the foregoing being the reason for the statement He's about to emphatically land upon: *"do not be anxious about tomorrow, for tomorrow will be anxious for itself."* Will your life tomorrow be without potential cause for worry? No, says Jesus, not at all. But, according to Him, according to the God who walked the earth as

a Man, tomorrow and the next day and the rest of your life are now without *reason* to worry. You belong to Him, now and forever. And, each day, every day, you are "His personal concern" (1 Peter 5:7 Phillips). *"Sufficient for the day is its own trouble."* And sufficient for that trouble is your God and His provision.

Now, shall we go live this way today?
I'd invite you—let's.

In Him, the Impossible
Is Possible

Promise
27

"Behold, I am the Lord, the God of all flesh. Is there anything too difficult for Me?"

JEREMIAH 32:27 BSB

Personally, I can't recall another question spoken in the Scriptures that holds the same meaning and weight as the question with which this implied promise concludes: "Is there anything too difficult for Me?" Because if there's any doubt in our minds as to God's ability to encounter, overcome and, even, demolish any difficulty, then—what are we doing? Who do we think we're going to follow, next, if this One, this God, can't surmount any challenge, hardship, barrier, or impasse?

My friend, I want you to truly know this God, this One, *"the Lord, the God of all flesh"* who is unstoppable in face of difficulty. I want you so unshakably resolved upon His power and sheer dynamism that there's never any more question for you in your day-to-day.

So, for that reason, I want to take you on a journey of His ability, over the eons, to overcome every difficulty, every trial, every divide, every impossibility that might've seemed insurmountable. And to do that, I want us to consider, in each era or day, His and our state of existence—*who He was* and who we were—during that precise period of time.

Consider:

Before Creation—God was. We weren't. He existed and we didn't exist at all. And yet He manifested existence and time and space and being, and made the triune choice to create us *"in His image."*

In the Garden of Eden—He was. We were now also. And He overcame any potential boundary lying between the Divine and those made-in-the-image-of-the-Divine, and He walked with us *"in the garden in the cool of the day"* (Genesis 3:8 ESV).

From the Fall until the Incarnation—He was God: perfect and holy. We were fallen: imperfect and broken. And yet, for the remainder of human history until His coming, He continued to manifest His grace and reveal His voice across the divide. It was only by His grace that "history" didn't end with the Fall. He might've scrapped the whole thing because humanity was no longer perfect.

The Incarnation—He was Himself *and yet with us.* We were still imperfect *and yet with Him.* He actually allowed humanity to see the very face of God.

The Cross—He was Himself *and yet totally in our sinful place, on our behalf.* We were our broken selves, *and yet our sin-existence hung suspended-in-time upon that Man on the Cross.* And He personally overcame sin, the separating force that had destroyed mankind ever since the Fall in the Garden of Eden.

The Resurrection—He was alive again, God and Man, entirely by His own volitional power. We were still imperfect, and yet now offered a new sinless, deathless, human existence. And He had permanently, once for all time, overcome death, *"the last enemy"* of mankind (1 Corinthians 15:26 NIV).

The Ascension—He was Himself, Man and God, upon the throne again. We were able, by His blood, to have direct access to that throne. And nothing can now separate our confident earth-to-Heaven approach: He has said, *"It is finished"* to all human-to-God separation.

Pentecost until today—He is with the Father and with us, within our hearts. We are here on earth as new Kingdom creations—and yet *"raised up with Christ and seated with him in the heavenly realms"* (Ephesians 2:6 NIV). His and our shared, bi-locational reality means there's no difficulty unable to be overcome, no provision meant to be unmet, no spiritual deficit He won't personally invade, overwhelm, and conquer. He is there and here; we are here and there.

My friend, in every portion of history and pre-history, we have dealt with the God who is unable to be stopped, unable to encounter any natural or supernatural difficulty that has any ounce of power against Him. Let us say to our hearts today, "Behold, I am following the Lord, the God of all flesh; nothing is too difficult for Him!"

- Lack of seeming substance? *He created existence!*

- Lack of connection? *He personally came to encounter us!*

- Lack of holiness? *He will never stop pursuing His people!*

- Lack of understanding of God? *He has showed us His face!*

- Fear of the consequences of sin? *He ended it!*

- Fear in the face of death? *He conquered it forever!*

- Desire to know God? *He invites you into the throne room of Heaven!*

- Desire for a new life? *He invites Himself right into your heart!*

Let me type it out again, with confidence, from me to you—Behold, you and I are following the Lord, the God of all flesh; nothing in the heavens or the earth is too difficult for Him!

Promise
28

"What men find impossible is perfectly possible with God."

Luke 18:27 Phillips

Today, I want to juxtapose five human situations—five little "impossible" vignettes—with their "perfectly possible" eventual God outcomes. And I won't tell you what they are beforehand; just get yourself pulled into each scene and be reminded of what our God can do.

Is your imagination ready?

One

You are standing on the gravelly, sandy shore of a body of water, looking across its depths to a far-distant shoreline. It is twilight. The stars are beginning to spread across the reaches of the sky; black night will be oncoming soon. Around you, thousands and thousands of people stretch along the coast, doing the exact same thing you are—looking out over the water, wishing something miraculous were possible rather than the slaughter you're beginning to expect.

Because, turning around, a mighty army stands at your rear, waiting to attack your people at the first morning light.

Their chariots and infantry stand row on row; Pharaoh's regalia gleaming in the last light of the evening.

What should you do?

What can you do?

Which, even as you're thinking that, is the moment when the cloud-pillar swings from front to back of all your people, your nation. Then, as you watch it settle between you and the Egyptian army, an east wind begins to blow over the Red Sea.

Two

You are standing in the first morning light, stretching your arms above your head, preparing to draw water from the well down the way. The eastern sky is brightening rapidly. As you grab your bucket and start to walk down the narrow trail, you are thinking of—

What's that?

Over there!

Your eyes have detected all kinds of movement on the range of hills that surrounds the small city in which you're standing. There shouldn't be people up there.

You look more closely.

Straining your eyes, you begin to see that everywhere—on all the hills—down every gully and approach—ride and march the massed armies of the King of Aram. The King of Aram is the personal enemy of your master. Your master is Elisha, the prophet of God.

Running inside, you shake him awake, shouting in his face for him to come and see the devastation that awaits you both. Slowly he gets out of bed, walks to the door and outside.

Then, blinking his eyes, doing a similar stretch to the one you'd been doing just minutes ago, he yawns loudly and then says to you, "Don't be afraid. Those who are with us are more than those who are with them."[1]

And before you can even ask what he means by such a preposterous statement of seeming untruth, he is lifting his hands to Heaven and entreating Yahweh: "Open his eyes, Lord, so that he may see."

And when you look again at the very same hills, valleys, gullies, and approaches, they are full of flaring, flashing horses, chariots, and armies made entirely of heavenly fire.

Three

You are standing in the open air, in front of the Temple, listening to the king of Judah praying aloud: *"Lord, the God of our ancestors, are you not the God who is in heaven? You rule over all the kingdoms of the nations. Power and might are in your hand, and no one can withstand you. ...But now here are men from Ammon, Moab and Mount Seir, whose territory you would not allow Israel to invade when they came from Egypt; so they turned away from them and did not destroy them. See how they are repaying us by coming to drive us out of the possession you gave us as an inheritance. Our God, will you not judge them? For we have no power to face this vast army that is attacking us. We do not know what to do, but our eyes are on you."[2]*

You turn and look out. Sure enough, across the far hills and over the plains of the middle-distance march the rank and file of Moab, Ammon, and the Meunites, with gleaming general staffs arrayed behind them. The sound of their march echoes into the city.

Another man has risen to speak to your king, *"Listen, King Jehoshaphat and all who live in Judah and Jerusalem! This is what the Lord says to you: 'Do not be afraid or discouraged because of this vast army. For the battle is not yours, but God's. Tomorrow march down against them. ...You will not have to fight this battle. Take up your positions; stand firm and see the deliverance the Lord will give you, Judah and Jerusalem. Do not be afraid; do not be discouraged. Go out to face them tomorrow, and the Lord will be with you.'"*[3]

In the morning, when you come to report for the march out—carrying your best sword and armor and buckler—you are told to go put those away. The king tells you, "Today, you will march out in worship. You will lead the army, in song, into the Lord's battle...."

Four

You are standing facing the mighty king of Babylon who asks, *"Is it true, Shadrach, Meshach and Abednego, that you do not serve my gods or worship the image of gold I have set up? Now when you hear the sound of the horn, flute, zither, lyre, harp, pipe and all kinds of music, if you are ready to fall down and worship the image I made, very good. But if you do not worship it, you will be thrown immediately into a blazing furnace. Then what god will be able to rescue you from my hand?"*[4]

You and your two friends look at each other. Your resolution is identical, and unchanged.

"King Nebuchadnezzar, we do not need to defend ourselves before you in this matter. If we are thrown into the blazing furnace, the God we serve is able to deliver us from it, and he will deliver us from Your Majesty's hand. But even if he does not, we want you to

know, Your Majesty, that we will not serve your gods or worship the image of gold you have set up."[5]

Within mere moments, you and your friends are standing before the open mouth of the furnace, feeling the exhalation of its impossibly hot heat. To your right and left are soldiers rapidly dying as the heat becomes so hot that they're literally melting away in their armor. The three of you move forward of your own accord. You are ready now to enter the flames.

For, inside, you've all caught sight of a Man, robed in the splendors of the heavenly throne room, beckoning you inside to fellowship.

Five

You are standing in the middle of a small town, in the center of a mid-sized district, in the heart of a subjugated, enslaved nation of your people. Your entire life has been lived under the yoke of Roman power and taxation; you know of no other masters, in your lifetime, than these greedy, grasping brutes.

And, on the other hand, in the place where past generations would've put their hope in God, their trust in Yahweh, you have only, ever, found Him to be silent. For almost four hundred years, you and your people haven't heard a whisper or a word that there is Anyone residing past the darkness stretching beyond tonight's stars.

That is, until earlier tonight.

In the eastern meadows, stretched out on your back, you and your friends had been accosted by an army of angelic beings! You had been told that God Himself was in your town, in your district, at the heart of your subjugated, enslaved nation of people!

So now you are in the town, walking toward the open mouth of the cave-stalls behind the inn, where the faintest light is flickering within.

From inside, you begin to hear the cry of a newborn baby.

Tears fill your eyes. "God with us," you whisper.

*   *   *

My friend, no matter what today holds—whether it's perfectly delightful or seemingly impossible—this is the God you've come to trust, and to follow. This is the One who—no matter what sort of impossibility is arrayed before you today—*is always with you.*

So, along with Moses, Elisha, Jehoshaphat, Shadrach, Meshach, Abednego, and the shepherds of Bethlehem, I'd remind you of His words once again: *"What men find impossible is perfectly possible with God."*

Amen and amen.

Endnotes

1. 2 Kings 6:16 NIV.

2. 2 Chronicles 20:6,10-12 NIV.

3. 2 Chronicles 20:15-17 NIV.

4. Daniel 3:14-15 NIV.

5. Daniel 3:16-18 NIV.

Promise
29

"For with God nothing will be impossible."

Luke 1:37 NKJV

In this second-to-last promise before the ending of our journey together, I'm going to break the cardinal rule of said journey: I'm going to use a promise not spoken directly from the lips of God, but one spoken *from* Him by His messenger-angel to Mary. And because we are almost to the end of these meditations and because I'm already breaking my own rule, I've decided to go big on breaking that rule. I'm already cracking the door by giving a promise not exactly from the mouth of God, so why not flood this day with other promises ascribed to His goodness?

So, sit back, take a deep breath, prepare your heart and mind, and understand that these are promises imparted to you by none other than the God of the universe. Let them be a declaration over your life.

> *There is therefore now no condemnation for those who are in Christ Jesus. For the law of the Spirit of life has set you free in Christ Jesus from the law of sin and death. For God has done what the law, weakened by*

the flesh, could not do. By sending his own Son in the likeness of sinful flesh and for sin, he condemned sin in the flesh, in order that the righteous requirement of the law might be fulfilled in us, who walk not according to the flesh but according to the Spirit (Romans 8:1-4 ESV).

...if you confess with your mouth that Jesus is Lord and believe in your heart that God raised him from the dead, you will be saved. For with the heart one believes and is justified, and with the mouth one confesses and is saved. For the Scripture says, "Everyone who believes in him will not be put to shame." For there is no distinction between Jew and Greek; for the same Lord is Lord of all, bestowing his riches on all who call on him. For "everyone who calls on the name of the Lord will be saved" (Romans 10:9-13 ESV).

He does not deal with us according to our sins, nor repay us according to our iniquities. For as high as the heavens are above the earth, so great is his steadfast love toward those who fear him; as far as the east is from the west, so far does he remove our transgressions from us (Psalm 103:10-12 ESV).

Therefore, brothers and sisters, since we have confidence to enter the Most Holy Place by the blood of Jesus, by a new and living way opened for us through the curtain, that is, his body, and since we have a great priest over the house of God, let us draw near to God with a sincere heart and with the full assurance that faith brings, having our hearts sprinkled to cleanse us from a guilty conscience and having our bodies washed with pure water. Let us hold unswervingly to the hope we profess, for he who promised is faithful (Hebrews 10:19-23 NIV).

For the Son of God, Jesus Christ, whom we proclaimed among you...was not Yes and No, but in him it is always Yes. For all the promises of God find their Yes in him. That is why it is through him that we utter our Amen to God for his glory. And it is God who establishes us with you in Christ, and has anointed us, and who has also put his seal on us and given us his Spirit in our hearts as a guarantee (2 Corinthians 1:19-22 ESV).

Likewise the Spirit helps us in our weakness. For we do not know what to pray for as we ought, but the Spirit himself intercedes for us with groanings too deep for words. And he who searches hearts knows what is the mind of the Spirit, because the Spirit intercedes for the saints according to the will of God. And we know that for those who love God all things work together for good, for those who are called according to his purpose. For those whom he foreknew he also predestined to be conformed to the image of his Son, in order that he might be the firstborn among many brothers. And those whom he predestined he also called, and those whom he called he also justified, and those whom he justified he also glorified (Romans 8:26-30 ESV).

His divine power has granted to us all things that pertain to life and godliness, through the knowledge of him who called us to his own glory and excellence, by which he has granted to us his precious and very great promises, so that through them you may become par-takers of the divine nature, having escaped from the corruption that is in the world because of sinful desire (2 Peter 1:3-4 ESV).

You keep him in perfect peace whose mind is stayed on you, because he trusts in you. Trust in the Lord for-ever, for the Lord God is an everlasting rock (Isaiah 26:3-4 ESV).

If any of you lacks wisdom, let him ask God, who gives generously to all without reproach, and it will be given him (James 1:5 ESV).

For we are his workmanship, created in Christ Jesus for good works, which God prepared beforehand, that we should walk in them (Ephesians 2:10 ESV).

I will bless the Lord at all times; his praise shall con-tinually be in my mouth. My soul makes its boast in the Lord; let the humble hear and be glad. Oh, mag-nify the Lord with me, and let us exalt his name together! I sought the Lord, and he answered me and delivered me from all my fears. Those who look to him are radiant, and their faces shall never be ashamed (Psalm 34:1-5 ESV).

But if we walk in the light, as he is in the light, we have fellowship with one another, and the blood of Jesus his Son cleanses us from all sin. If we say we have no sin, we deceive ourselves, and the truth is not in us. If we confess our sins, he is faithful and just to forgive us our sins and to cleanse us from all unrighteousness (1 John 1:7-9 ESV).

...you know in your hearts and souls, all of you, that not one word has failed of all the good things that the Lord your God promised concerning you. All have come to pass for you; not one of them has failed (Joshua 23:14 ESV).

And my God will supply every need of yours according to his riches in glory in Christ Jesus. To our God and Father be glory forever and ever. Amen (Philippians 4:19-20 ESV).

We are afflicted in every way, but not crushed; perplexed, but not driven to despair; persecuted, but not forsaken; struck down, but not destroyed; always carrying in the body the death of Jesus, so that the life of Jesus may also be manifested in our bodies. For we who live are always being given over to death for Jesus' sake, so that the life of Jesus also may be manifested in our mortal flesh (2 Corinthians 4:8-11 ESV).

What then shall we say to these things? If God is for us, who can be against us? He who did not spare his own Son but gave him up for us all, how will he not also with him graciously give us all things? Who shall bring any charge against God's elect? It is God who justifies. Who is to condemn? Christ Jesus is the one who died—more than that, who was raised—who is at the right hand of God, who indeed is interceding for us (Romans 8:31-34 ESV).

Here's my prayer as I finish reading through all those promise Scriptures:

Jesus, there You are—at the right hand of God, interceding for us. Thank You. Thank You for dying for us. Thank You that You are manifesting Your own life through our lives; that You provide for us; that You never ever fail us. Thank You also that You are just, yet forgive us for our sins, and that we never need to feel ashamed again. Thank You that You are shaping us, making us Your work-manship, aligning our lives with Your Way—which You have already prepared. Thank You that Your wisdom and Your peace are only as far away as asking for them, every single day.

Thank You that we may partake of Your nature by receiving Your very Spirit and that that Spirit is within us, praying for us. Thank You for being the glorious "Yes" of Heaven, the great High Priest of Heaven, One who doesn't deal with us according to our sins. Thank You for Your wondrous, glorious grace, Jesus. For there is now no condemnation for we who are in You—thank You! The law of the Spirit has set us free, in you, from the law of sin and death—thank You! For You have done what the law, weakened by the flesh, could not do—You did it, Jesus! You came in the likeness of sinful flesh and for sin; You condemned sin in the flesh, and now the righteous requirement of the law can be fulfilled in us, who may now walk not according to the flesh but according to Your Spirit. We are walking now in Your Spirit, Jesus. Thank You for all that You've personally done for us.

We love You.

Amen.

Section Seven

HE WILL RETURN

Promise
30

"Let not your hearts be troubled. Believe in God; believe also in me. In my Father's house are many rooms. If it were not so, would I have told you that I go to prepare a place for you? And if I go and prepare a place for you, I will come again and will take you to myself, that where I am you may be also. And you know the way to where I am going.' ...Jesus said to him, 'I am the way, and the truth, and the life. No one comes to the Father except through me.'"

JOHN 14:1-4,6 ESV

Whenever I think of the return of Jesus—of that Beginning of the Beginning and the End of Ends—my mind often goes to a man whose story lies at the very opening of this whole glorious drama. His name is Enoch, and this is what we're told of him:

When Enoch had lived 65 years, he became the father of Methuselah. After he became the father of Methuselah, Enoch walked faithfully with God 300 years and had other sons and daughters. Altogether, Enoch lived a total of 365 years. Enoch walked faithfully with God; then he was no more, because God took him away (Genesis 5:21-24 NIV).

Naturally, it's that last sentence that grabs one's attention. The idea of *"walking faithfully with God"* we can readily understand; but we tend to sit up in our chairs when we hear of a heavenly disappearing act that is borne from that faithfulness—an evasion of death because of God whisking someone away in His wondrous train. I've often imagined that, while walking faithfully with God one afternoon enjoying the splendors of yet another day of enjoying Him, Enoch just suddenly found himself in Heaven! And looking around, getting his bearings, seeing the God who he'd so faithfully walked with so long, he could only laugh and say, with a shake of his head, *"You!"*

So, why am I talking about Enoch with this final promise?

Because the only way to live with untroubled hearts, believing in God, believing in Jesus; the only way to wait upon our eventual placement in the place He has for us in Heaven; the only way to be watchful for His coming again—His great taking of us to Himself, to His Father, to Heaven—*is to walk faithfully with Him today.* To rise out of bed, brush your teeth, get dressed, get ready, get fed, get out the door to work, get home, get in your routine, get back in bed—*all with Him.* To let every hour of your day be one in fellowship *with Him.* To let *Him* become the rhythm of your days. To finally, firmly understand that there's *absolutely nothing higher* for your human life than to walk in intimacy with Jesus of Nazareth. And to so do, just like Enoch did.

When Jesus earlier described the times of His return, He put it this way:

> *There will be signs in the sun and moon and stars, and on the earth there will be dismay among the nations and bewilderment at the roar of the surging sea. Men's courage will fail completely as they realise what is threatening the world, for the very powers of heaven will be shaken. Then men will see the Son of Man coming in a cloud with great power and splendour! But when these things begin to happen, look up, hold your heads high, for you will soon be free* (Luke 21:25-28 Phillips).

My friend, the reality of the mystery of the Return of Jesus is that, being totally unknown in its timing, *it could be today!* We might be going about the business of our mundane little routine this afternoon and—looking up—*it's happening!* Jesus Himself, descending in the same glory in which He once ascended, coming again to take us away, as He promised!

How would He find you?

How would He find me?

With *"heads held high"* and *"free"*?

His best friend, the apostle John, writing many years after the Ascension, captured the spirit I would like to see in myself that day. This is how I'd want to be if Jesus happened to decide to return during this particular afternoon:

> *...Here and now we are God's children. We don't know what we shall become in the future. We only*

know that, if reality were to break through, we should reflect his likeness, for we should see him as he really is! (1 John 3:2 Phillips)

What a thought! That, today, being a son of God, not entirely knowing where my life is going, I can rest assured that, *"if reality were to break through"* this very afternoon, He would recognize me and I would finally, fully see Him!

The highest prayer I can pray for your life—and the reason I've taken the time to write these words—is that you'd begin to see your individual life as the place of Jesus' greatest joy, and that Jesus Himself would overtake everything for you. That perhaps, someday, the following might be written of you:

When they had lived a certain number of years, they became, fully and consciously, a child of God. And after they became this son or daughter of God, they walked faithfully with God every day of their life and helped others to become children of God. Altogether, they walked with God every remaining year of their life, all 365 days of each one. They walked faithfully with God; then they were no more—or Jesus returned—and God took them away.

One day, while *"walking faithfully with God,"* enjoying the splendors of yet another day of enjoying Him, either Jesus will return, or you will suddenly find yourself in Heaven! And looking around, getting your bearings, seeing the God who you've so enjoyed walking with for so long, you'll laugh and start to say, *"You!"*

But, even better, Jesus will beat you to the punch.

With that love in His glorious eyes, brimming over with tears of joy that you're finally, eternally together forever, He'll whisper, *"You!"*

Jesus, we await You today in the joy of Your presence. Come, Lord Jesus, come!

About Eugene Luning

Eugene Luning directs *The Union*, a ministry of teaching, speaking, retreats, podcasting and spiritual counseling. His overriding passion is speaking of Jesus.

Eugene graduated from Westmont College in Santa Barbara, California, and, before that, received his preparatory education at John Burroughs School in St. Louis, Missouri. Prior to his work with The Union, Eugene syndicated commercial real estate transactions in California and the Midwest, and also served for a number of years with the youth ministry, Young Life.

Eugene and his wife, Jenny, are the parents of three children, Hadley, Tripp, and Hoyt. They live in Colorado Springs, Colorado.

www.ingramcontent.com/pod-product-compliance
Lightning Source LLC
Chambersburg PA
CBHW070038100426
42740CB00013B/2723